DESERT
SORROWS

DESERT
SORROWS

Poems by Tayseer al-Sboul

Translated by Nesreen Akhtarkhavari and Anthony A. Lee

Michigan State University Press • East Lansing

This book was published with support by The Honorary Consul General
of Jordan in Chicago, Mr. Ihsan Sweis.

♻ The paper used in this publication meets the minimum requirements
of ANSI/NISO Z39.48-1992 (R 1997) (Permanence of Paper).

Michigan State University Press
East Lansing, Michigan 48823-5245

Printed and bound in the United States of America.

21 20 19 18 17 16 15   1 2 3 4 5 6 7 8 9 10

LIBRARY OF CONGRESS CATALOGING-IN-PUBLICATION DATA

Sabul, Taysir.

Desert sorrows : poems / by Tayseer al-Sboul ;

translated by Nesreen Akhtarkhavari and Anthony A. Lee.

pages cm

English-Arabic edition of: Ahzan sahrawiyah.

Includes bibliographical references.

ISBN 978-1-61186-161-7 (pbk. : alk. paper)—ISBN 978-1-60917-449-1 (pdf)

I. Akhtarkhavari, Nesreen, translator. II. Lee, Anthony A., 1947– translator.

III. Sabul, Taysir. Poems. Selections. English. IV. Sabul, Taysir. Poems. Selections. V. Title.

PJ7862.A2834A2 2015

892.7'16—dc23

2014043272

Book design by Charlie Sharp, Sharp Des!gns, Lansing, MI
Cover design by Shaun Allshouse, www.shaunallshouse.com

Michigan State University Press is a member of the Green Press Initiative and is
committed to developing and encouraging ecologically responsible publishing
practices. For more information about the Green Press Initiative and the use
of recycled paper in book publishing, please visit *www.greenpressinitiative.org.*

Visit Michigan State University Press at *www.msupress.org*

CONTENTS

PROLOGUE

Otaba Al-Sboul

The most incomprehensible thing about the universe is that it is comprehensible.

—*Albert Einstein*

Some people believe that everything about our universe, no matter how esoteric or counterintuitive, is knowable. I wish I were able to state the same about my father!

In mid-January, 1939, in a remote, forgotten small town in a southern Emirate of Transjordan called Tafilah (30.84° N, 35.6° E)—or "Tafileh" per T. E. Lawrence's *Seven Pillars of Wisdom*—a baby boy was born to a septuagenarian father. Expected to bring blessings and happiness, he was given the name Tayseer, which can be interpreted as "made easy" or "soften."

Being the youngest amongst four male siblings granted him some privilege, as he was spared the hard work of farming the family's rugged land. Having free time for contemplation might have played a role in shaping Tayseer's future poetic spirit and unique psychological fabric.

I believe Americans are blessed with many fortunes. No doubt one of these is that they have been saved from dealing with a lengthy history that weighs heavy on the shoulders of the present. They don't have to deal with the memory of lengthy feuds and of empires disintegrating, leaving scars behind them. In the twentieth century, the Middle and Near East were going through a tough transition after the Arab Revolt against the Ottoman Empire (1916–1918). In the aftermath, there was a lot of disappointment aimed at allied forces' promises (including short-lived euphoria over U.S. President Wilson's Fourteen Points), which fell short of meeting aspirations to create sovereign nations and states.

Back in the forties and fifties, the region, which can even outclass Crete in "producing more history than it can consume locally" (to paraphrase Saki) was feeling the flames of colliding ideologies, the burden of legacies, and interest from superpowers, which began mainly after oil discovery in the Persian Gulf. The tension also was fueled by the establishment of the Israeli state in 1948, which has produced endless political and military frictions since.

Tayseer was influenced by all of that. His exceptional literary capabilities surfaced at an early age, but intrinsic personal traits also played a critical role in shaping his works and his perception of the world. Being emotionally sensitive and perfectionist, his harsh self-criticism led him to destroy much of his finished and unfinished work, leaving us with his sole poetry divan (*Desert Sorrows*), a single novel (*You as of Today*), two short stories, and a number of scholarly articles and reviews.

Tayseer was always searching; his journey included the quest for human and social meaning. As a teen, he joined a pan-Arab Baa'th party (which promised the grandiose dream of unifying Arabs, who are dispersed today between twenty plus countries in the Middle East and Africa), to be expelled later while studying law in Damascus, Syria, after criticizing ideological aspects and party positions. (Interestingly enough this happened in 1961, even before the party came to power in Iraq and Syria.)

Tayseer's professional career also spanned across multiple jobs, including short stints in Bahrain and Saudi Arabia before he returned to Jordan, where he settled into the newly established field of radio broadcast.

Tayseer's interests were multifaceted. He was big fan of great writers' works; my mother described how deeply touched he was by Ernest Hemingway's suicide in 1961. Further, at times he was almost obsessed with literature like "The Decline of the West," by Oswald Spengler, and T. S. Eliot's "The Waste Land."

He was an opponent of U.S. policies in the Middle East and Vietnam but a big admirer of the American space program. (He woke me up, a six-year-old boy in 1972, to watch one of Apollo's missions, transmitted by a Jordanian official TV channel.)

With his life consumed with literature and politics and the dream of a great nation, I sometimes find it amazing that he managed to marry my mother (May Al Yateem) and have two children (me and my sister, Saba).

On Thursday, November 15, 1973, around 1:45, Tayseer decided he could not take what was happening anymore and committed suicide.

The date coincides with the meeting of the Israelis and the Egyptian after the October War, also known as the Yom Kippur War or the Ramadan War, where Egypt and Syria launched attacks jointly on Israel. Early euphoria over swift victories for the Egyptian and Syrian forces turned out to be premature, as Israel managed not only to contain its first-ever Arab-initiated massive attack but also to launch successful counterattack, trapping the Egyptian Third Army and coming within a few kilometers of both the Syrian capital Damascus and the Egyptian capital Cairo. Like many in his generation, he saw the meeting between the Israelis and the Egyptian as the culmination of Arab defeat.

My father's tragic end left deep scars on my family, especially my mother, leaving us with nothing but the need to find our path to consolation and reconciliation. On a personal note, I cannot claim that I have managed to fully get over it.

When the Jordanian Writers Society approached us requesting permission for Nesreen Akhtarkhavari to translate Tayseer's novel, we had some doubts. The task is quite challenging, as the novel is full of regional historical context and deep religious and cultural references that make it very difficult for readers lacking knowledge about its background to fully comprehend the text. Akhtarkhavari not only proved to be up to the challenge, but exceeded our expectations. Encouraged by the very positive reviewer responses to the translation, she next translated Tayseer's other short stories. Then she collaborated with the American poet Anthony Lee to translate the collection of poems found in *Desert Sorrows*, which is a challenging work as well. To both of them, I would like to extend my deep and sincere appreciation for investing time and efforts into translating my father's works, and to Michigan State University Press for publishing this book.

In a region where history seems to be dormant and the present tends to be static and unchanging, the spring of 2011 held a surprise for many observers and analysts of the Arab world. In a matter of weeks, two relatively successful and stable regimes toppled, in Tunisia and Egypt, followed by unrest in other Arab countries. The whole region seems to have reached a tipping point with no return. To the outside world, this foreign region seems to be the center of total chaos, violence, and confusion. But there is more to Arabs than that.

By sharing Tayseer's works with Western readers, we hope that a new channel of communication between our worlds is establish, and that his voice stand as a witness to our commonality as a human race.

TRANSLATING TAYSEER

Anthony A. Lee

Before I began working on this translation of the poems of Tayseer al-Sboul, I knew nothing at all about the man. Google searches yielded almost no information. I did learn that he was a Jordanian writer who had committed suicide at an early age. But one web page referred to him as "she," rather than "he," which only confused the matter. So, as I approached the translations of the Arabic poems provided to me by Nesreen Akhtarkhavari, I had practically no context in which to understand them. I simply decided that whatever I was going to learn about Tayseer's life I would have to learn from his poems.

The first poem I read was "Desert Sorrows (1)," which is also the first selection in this book. Even though Akhtarkhavari was fascinated by the poem, I first didn't find much there. It seemed to me, from my American perspective, that the poem fell flat. The images of the desert were too clichéd, and the narrative seemed too stereotyped to represent the author's real experience:

> From time before time,
> in the darkest caves of eternity,
> it stretched through the Arabian Desert,
> flowing like a dream, magic, melancholy,
> like the nights of Scheherazade.

I tried to find something there. Frankly, I couldn't. But I missed the point.

The second poem I read seemed more like the poetry I knew. "Winter Will Not End," clearly written at the end of a failed relationship, would be familiar territory to any modern poet. Tayseer captures his feelings of sadness and regret in a few words. But then, as I read on, the poem became something else:

> Winter has ended.
> Boredom has ended.
> I know I love the spring.

I long for it with desire.
But my suffering heart, full of winter,
. . . .
appears at no fixed season.
. . . .
My life is winter.

Suddenly, the poem unfolded and caught me in its grip. Immediately I recognized Tayseer's description of my own lifelong struggle with depression. I stared at the lines and discovered something about myself that I had not known before. "My life is winter." The poem had conjured up a magic that only a poet can perform: an apocalypse (from Greek *apokalypsis*, from *apokalyptein*: to uncover), a revelation. A line of poetry is spoken and it becomes real.

As I continued to read the poems and to work with them for this book, I found many such lines. I developed a deep identification with and attachment to the young Tayseer, who was a poet, like myself. He had lived through the same ages and life stages that I had experienced. He had sought to tackle the same terrible contradictions in the world that I had. He had struggled with evil and injustice, as I had. And he had found no resolution, as I had found none. Though separated by time and space, though living in different cultures, with different politics, and speaking different languages, I shared his struggle and his sadness. I recognized in him my own failure to find what Tayseer calls "the impossible":

I am still searching,
suffering,
trying to catch the impossible.

Others might call it a search for inner peace, a search for social justice, a search for goodness, a search for salvation. I knew exactly what he meant. His search was my search.

This book is an attempt to translate the poems of Tayseer al-Sboul into English in language that will accomplish the same thing he was able to accomplish in Arabic, that will allow the reader to connect with the poet as I was able to connect with him—on a deep, personal, and intimate level. In such a quest, a word-for-word translation is no help at all, and this book makes no attempt at that. The challenge for any translation of poetry is to bring a poem from one language and culture into another language and culture, while remaining true to both the spirit and the meaning of the original. A translation of only the meaning of the words might provide a fairly thorough explanation of the sense of a poem, but it likely contains little of the beauty, the pathos, or the excitement of the original. The worst result of translating a poem would be to take something that sounds urgent, natural, and real in the original language and render it into English that is dull, convoluted, and uninteresting. The goal of this English edition is to translate Tayseer by crafting lines that hold up as English poems on their own merits, while remaining as close and true in form and meaning to the Arabic originals as possible.

The conversion of poetry presents unique and seemingly insurmountable challenges for any translator. On the face of it, translating a poem from one language to another seems impossible. How can a poem be translated? That super-condensed form of language that captures the essence of our experience, which must appeal to the mind as much as the emotions, in images and words embedded with a deep cultural value on multiple levels and with multiple meanings. Even substituting a few words in the same language could destroy the poem and ruin its effect. How then can all the words of a poem be changed for words in a different language, with their foreign connotations and associations, and preserve anything of the original?

On the other hand, what is poetry, after all? Poetry is not words. It is the language that we turn to when mere words cannot express our thoughts and feelings. Poetry is, in fact, an attempt to move beyond language, to communicate states of mind and states of spirit that cannot be conveyed conversationally but that nonetheless must be expressed. A poem uses more than words to capture an emotion or an existential state in words. It can only point toward—or evoke, or perhaps uncover—such a state. If it doesn't do this, then the poem is a failure. So, perhaps it is possible—across languages, across cultures, across time—to translate poems that will evoke an apocalypse in a new audience.

We find that by some miracle of language this is possible. Though to make this happen, the translators must struggle to find the concepts, the music, and the images in a new language that can be crafted to the same effect as the original poems.

The reader may be curious about the methods we used, especially considering I know no Arabic at all. Akhtarkhavari initially translated each of these poems into English, preserving Tayseer's original lines and voice. Then I took those lines and slightly modified them when needed to ensure that they were acceptable poems in English without altering the intent of the poet. My first edits were then returned to Akhtarkhavari for comment and correction. And then we went back and forth from there until both of us were satisfied with the outcome. The act of "translating" is nuanced through this process. The meaning of the translated Arabic impresses itself on the consciousness of the English poet who seeks to ensure that the words and images in the new language are as clear and powerful as those in the original. The meaning of the poem is ensured by the Arabic speaker, while the clarity and power of the poem is confirmed by the English poet.

Of course, the quality of the resulting translation depends upon both the knowledge of the scholar and the skill of the poet. This method of translation is relatively new to academia, which has traditionally relied on the unassisted language scholar to provide the translations of poetic texts. The results were often criticized, especially by poets and native speakers, as wooden and awkward, providing little insight into the beauty or the appeal of the originals. This kind of collaboration between scholar and poet was pioneered by Amin Banani and Jascha Kessler, with their translations of the poems of the modern Iranian poet Forugh Farrokhzad.[1]

Amin Banani (1926–2013) was for many years a professor of Persian language and history at UCLA, and before his passing he was one of the foremost scholars of Persian literature in the United States. His decision to collaborate with an American poet on the translation of the poems of Forugh Farrokhzad was careful and considered. As he explained to me, it was the result of his dissatisfaction, and even frustration, with translations of Persian poetry accomplished by Persian scholars working alone. He felt that these translations were accurate but uninspired.

Banani was a brilliant scholar who understood that his translations of Farrokhzad's poems into English were not likely to employ language that would satisfy him or a larger Western audience. And so he sought out Kessler, a distinguished professor of English at UCLA and a poet in his own right. The insight that Banani had was simple but profound: Poems are written by poets. If he wanted to translate Persian poems for an American audience, he would have to collaborate with an English-speaking poet. He told me, by way of illustrating this point, that he had seen the title of Farrokhzad's famous poem (also the title of her last book), "Tavallodi digar," regrettably translated into English as "Another Birth." Though technically correct, he felt this phrase was simply inadequate. However, he was delighted with Kessler's insightful poetic translation "Born Again," which he used in their book.[2] Kessler's words captured the meaning of personal transformation that the poet had meant to convey.

I collaborated with Kessler and Banani some years later on the translation of a volume of the poems by another Iranian woman, the nineteenth-century poet Qurratu'l-'Ayn, also known as Táhirih.[3] In this case, two poets benefited from Banani's scholarship. The three of us went back and forth for two years, sometimes tussling over the words in English, to finally publish a book we could all be satisfied with. Later, I collaborated with Banani alone on a volume of translations of the short poems of Rumi.[4]

Tayseer's Quest

In reading Tayseer's work and working with Akhtarkhavari on finding ways to translate it into English poetry, I was repeatedly struck by two distinctive features that are found in all of his poems. One is his brutal honesty. Tayseer shares with us the most intimate and painful moments of his life. He never tries to hide his failures or his regrets. He never shrinks from self-criticism. We witness the full emotions of a human being. The other quality is his uncompromising and continuous struggle to find truth—his quest for "the impossible." He is determined to search for ultimate reality, the true essence of life, even if he knows he will never find it.

Speaking as a poet, and certainly not as an Arabic scholar, I can appreciate Tayseer's poetry as an important contribution to world literature. Tayseer—either knowingly or unknowingly—follows in the path of Faust in German folklore and in Goethe's classic epic. Faust is an educated intellectual who is unable to find happiness or fulfillment in life. He longs for more. The devil proposes a bargain: since Faust is bored, Mephistopheles promises to show him the endless range of earthly possibilities. He will guide him through an infinity of human experience, without end. But on one condition: Faust must never tire of his journey. In his famous lines, the devil warns Faust that if he says to his guide:

> Wait! Let me stay here.
> This is so beautiful.[5]

at that moment, his quest will end. Faust accepts.[6] Through Tayseer's poems, I followed him on his Faustian journey through the full range of human experience, though moments of joy and pain, of exultation and despair. No aspect of his life was held back. Everything was laid bare. As I swam deeper and deeper into Tayseer's poetic legacy, I could discern no pretense or dishonesty. He tore open his chest and gave me his heart. As was Faust, he was determined to face every facet of human life squarely, without losing courage. Like Faust, he found the journey impossible.

Tayseer's painful struggles with depression are sometimes personified as "winter." At times he welcomes the approach of winter, and occasionally we find him defeated by it. In "Moments of Wood" he is crushed by his depression on the evening of a Muslim festival. Just as easily, in "Pantheism" he captures the beauty of a mystical moment, a sort of beatific vision when he sees the unity of all creation and stares in wonder.

Tayseer openly writes about his sexuality. Tayseer's erotic imagery is unrestrained and explicit. In "Secrets" he recounts the story of one liaison—from the first sound of his lover's footsteps in the hallway at the secret rendezvous to his moment of physical ecstasy—holding back nothing. He also tells us of his unsuccessful quest for love and failed attempts to find happiness. His masterful poetic triptychs encapsulate the beginning, the middle, and the end of certain relationships with few words.

Tayseer's poems speak of his encounter with religion, his desire to continue experiencing life there. Here again, the legend of Faust resonates:

Forgive me,
I did not bury my forehead
in a turban.
No, and my conscience was not sacrificed
in a confession booth.
But I
have my rituals and prayers.[7]

Tayseer sometimes hears the voice of God. But that voice commands him to be silent and to merge into the traditional conformity of the masses:

I bargained with God for this. He said:
Go back to silence. The womb of silence is the only refuge
for eyes that stare out aimlessly.
I hesitated
and almost did it.[8]

To his credit, and to our great benefit, he didn't do it at that point. Rather, he chose life's struggles for a little longer and left us with the poetic testament of his strivings.

Tayseer writes of his political disappointments with the same honesty and tenderness with which he recounts his love affairs. I know nothing of what seems to have been Tayseer's encounter with the authorities, his persecution for his political convictions, the turmoil of his generation, his suffering, how he was forced to betray his comrades. But I found all these episodes in his poems, told with his characteristic honesty and openness, his refusal to be silenced. The poem "From a Sojourner," for example, speaks in tragic tones about his suffering and disappointments.

His mistreatment by authorities exceeded the limits of his endurance: he tells us that he was defeated. He confesses: "Under cracks of the whip I broke."[9] It appears that he gives up the names of his friends, and his betrayal haunts him for the rest of his life. In several poems he pleads his innocence, and in "A Piece of My Innocent Heart" he cries out:

> I know I crucified my brothers,
> my loved ones.
> I plead: Odysseus! Odysseus!
> You who unearthed our land,
> released its chained-up gifts,
> be generous. Give me two palms full of your tears.
> Wash away my sin.
> Lift from my tortured conscience
> the pain and burning of my soiling.

He calls not to God but to Odysseus, who was on his own seemingly endless journey, but who finally found his way home.

Tayseer's journey shows us war in poetry, as well. Of course, he lived through the 1967 Arab-Israeli war in which Jordan lost the West Bank. His poem "Terror" captures the horror and chaos of war as well as any poem could.

Tayseer many times finds himself torn between the lure of Western culture and civilization and the history of the Arab people. He was, of course, part of both worlds, and he could not choose between them. In "A Gypsy" he looks upon modern European and American culture as he found it in the night life of Beirut with horror:

> When the clubs crowd with mockery,
> with mechanical dolls dancing the tango,
> death creeps silently into the tango,
> and life disappears
> quietly.
> Gypsy!
> Bodies fall and die,
> quiver like slaughtered birds,
> like wind shaking leaves
> that fall when jazz blasts.

That dreadful trumpet,
hollering through the night into a dead crowd!
Would that I were blind
and deaf
before I witnessed the night of the dead.

Yet, in "Andalusian Song" Tayseer imagines the East and the West as two mistresses to which he is equally attracted. In this masterful poem, he cannot choose between them but can only stay drunk and cry. He is torn apart by his double identity. In this he gives voice to a whole generation of educated Jordanians who faced the same dilemma. It is the dilemma of all Arabs, all colonized people, who are similarly torn. The pain and terror of this situation was best described by W. E. B. Du Bois in his classic volume *The Souls of Black Folk,* written at the beginning of the twentieth century on the American continent but expressing the same hopeless state of "two-ness":

It is a peculiar sensation, this double-consciousness, this sense of always looking at one's self through the eyes of others, of measuring one's soul by the tape of a world that looks on in amused contempt and pity. One ever feels his two-ness,— . . . two souls, two thoughts, two unreconciled strivings; two warring ideals in one dark body, whose dogged strength alone keeps it from being torn asunder.[10]

Although Tayseer almost certainly never read this passage, it could have been written by Du Bois for him.

Another ubiquitous theme found in Tayseer's poetry is death. The portents of his suicide are found in many poems:

The song in my bones sings:
Here death is joy:
A pure, white glimmer that can't be touched
embraces the black.[11]

Death is everywhere—in the horror of war, in the gypsy's camp, in the city's clubs, in his room on the evening of a festival, in every "fleeting moment."

As I worked on Tayseer's poems, I came to know him as a friend and as a brother—in those moments, my closest friend and my true brother. Finally, I came to the translation of the last poem that Tayseer had written, in 1973, just before his suicide. "The Journey" is also the last poem in this collection. As I went over that translation, checking it for the final time, I cried. I couldn't help it. It was not a loud sobbing. There was no break in expression on my face. Mine was just a silent and involuntary tearing that I couldn't stop.

I wept. Sadness overwhelmed me. I wept for the pain of my friend, an agony from which he could never escape. I wept for the failure of his journey toward the infinite, for the emptiness he found at the end of life. As did Faust, Tayseer learned that the full range of human experience—when he faced it with honesty, refusing to submit, refusing to compromise, refusing to be satisfied with religion or with ideology—led him to discover that infinity of human shortcomings, too cruel, too harsh, too cold, too tearing, too dreary to accept and go on, even at the summit:

> and there the summit appears.
> He sees
> there is nothing there to see.
> There is nothing there to touch.
> The summit is just empty.
> He no longer needs people.
> He needs nothing.

So, I couldn't help it. I wept for the sadness of Tayseer's life, and for the sadness of my own.

I wept, I suppose, for the impossibility of the human condition, for the necessity and the tragedy of our endless strivings toward the summit.

NOTES

1. Forugh Farrokhzad, *Bride of Acacias: Selected Poems of Forugh Farrokhzad*, trans. Amin Banani and Jascha Kessler (Caravan Books, 1982).

2. Farrokhzad, *Bride of Acacias*, 11, 90.

3. Qurratu'l-ʿAyn, *Táhirih—A Portrait in Poetry: Selected Poems of Qurratu'l-ʿAyn*, trans. Amin Banani, Jascha Kessler, and Anthony A. Lee (Los Angeles: Kalimát Press, 2004).

4. Mevlana Rumi, *Rumi—53 Secrets from the Tavern of Love: Poems from the Rubiayat of Mevlana Rumi*, trans. Amin Banani and Anthony A. Lee (Ashland, OR: White Cloud Press, 2014).

5. This is the way the famous lines should be translated. Sometimes they are seen as: "O linger a while. / Thou art so fair."

6. The traditional legends celebrate the moment when Faust is finally dragged into hell. However, in Goethe's retelling of the tale, Faust is saved because of his commitment to the search for truth. The angels escorting him to heaven reply to the devil's complaints with the retort that: "Man must strive [in order to find salvation], and striving, he must err."

7. From "Unbearable Words."

8. From "Dust."

9. From "The Impossible."

10. W. E. B. Du Bois, "Of Our Spiritual Strivings," in *The Souls of Black Folk* (1903).

11. From "The Final Shore."

INTRODUCTION

Nesreen Akhtarkhavari

Tayseer al-Sboul not only is arguably Jordan's most acclaimed writer and poet, he also is, as has been often pointed out, one of the greatest Arab literary reformers, having written some of the most creative and sophisticated works in modern Arabic literature.[1] Furthermore, al-Sboul's work is a distinguished feature of Jordanian literature. We undoubtedly "cannot discuss Jordanian literature without discussing his creative experience."[2] Despite his short life (1939–1973), he managed to record with striking clarity a Jordanian narrative that told of the struggles, dreams, and aspirations of a young nation during some of its most defining periods.

In contrast to the large number of articles, commentaries, and studies of al-Sboul's life and work in Arabic, there is only one article about him in English: "Taysīr al-Subūl's *You As of Today* in a Post-Modernist Context" by Ahmad Y. Majdoubeh, which discusses Tayseer's work as the first postmodernist Arabic novel. In 2011 Wael Rabadi translated *You As of Today* into French with the support of the Jordanian Ministry of Culture. In 2012 the Jordanian Writers Society published my translation of the novel in English.

Desert Sorrows is the first translation of Tayseer's complete body of poetry into English. These thirty-six poems were written between 1960 and 1973 and originally published in *Ahzan Sahrawiyah* and *Tayseer Al-Sboul: Al-A'mal Al-Kamelah*.[3] The poems in *Desert Sorrows* are not ordered chronologically or according to the sequence in either of the Arabic publications. They are arranged under four major themes that tie the selections together. Special effort was exerted when translating the collection to stay as close as possible to the original poems' content and form while still producing meaningful and poetic verses in English.

The poems in the collection are written in modern free style. Tayseer abides by the taf'eelah—the basic unit of prosody in Arabic poetry—and employs a "circular" prosody, wherein the line does not consist of a discrete whole or a fixed number of taf'eelahs. In some cases he employs a more complex prosody, a structure borrowed from the traditional Arabic Qasida. As a result, his poems are melodic and full of internal rhythm and rhyme. The poems' imagery is derived from his local environment, and the symbolism is inspired mainly by Arab culture, literature, and tradition. This is a departure from the excessive use of ancient mythology that has been employed by many other contemporary Arab writers.

Most of al-Sboul's poems are sad and melancholic. This reflects his internal struggle and the general tone of the time he lived in, with its wars and social and political crises. Tayseer did not live in isolation but immersed himself in the issues that impacted his people and became consumed by them. By introducing al-Sboul's poems to the English reader, we hope to translate not only a unique poetic experience and the collective pain and anguish of a young Jordanian poet but also the experience of a generation attempting to cope with its changing world. In her introduction to a collection of al-Sboul's work, his wife, May Al-Yateem, wrote: "Tayseer's life moved through the same patterns that the youth of his generation went through, [with] the major events that took place in the Arab world shaping his life and directing it."[4] His dream was to carry the stamp of a great nation,[5] and to that, he dedicated his life and writings.

Jordan is notably present in the language, imagery, and content of Tayseer's poems, stories, and novel, where the personal and the public intertwine. His literature carries the scent of the place, as well as its history, geography, and the aspirations of its people. This, combined with the quality of his work and his honesty and willingness to share his unadulterated feelings and despair with readers, made Tayseer a national celebrity. To this day, events, articles, and news releases about his life and work mark the anniversary of his passing. The Jordanian Ministry of Culture and the Jordanian Writers Society continue to support new publications about al-Sboul and his work. In addition to printing translations of his novel in English and French,[6] in 2013, the Ministry of Culture reprinted an updated edition of Suliman al-Azrai's book about Tayseer.[7] In the same year, *Afkar*, the official journal of the Ministry, dedicated a complete volume to his life, including analysis of his work, reflection on his life by family and friends, and an article I wrote about American students' reflections and reactions to the English translation of his novel *You as of Today*.[8] Further, the Jordanian Writers Society sponsors an annual literary competition and award in his honor.

Tayseer al-Sboul was born and raised in Tafilah, a relatively remote agrarian village at the edge of the desert in southern Jordan. He grew up in a traditional middle-class family, as the youngest of nine siblings with an authoritative father strongly connected to his land and people. Despite his limited resources, Tayseer's father was keen on educating his children. Tayseer loved school and excelled. From an early age, his gift for writing poetry was recognized by his peers and teachers alike. He was frequently invited to recite his poems at school gatherings and public events. Before graduating from high school, Tayseer's work was published, and he won numerous awards for his writing, including one from a national competition sponsored by Radio Jordan.

Tayseer witnessed major changes that affected the region, was impacted by them, and later projected them into his work. He was only nine when the 1948 War erupted, but the sight of Palestinian refugees pouring into Jordan in a state of confusion, their makeshift accommodations and hope of returning home, was indelibly imprinted on the mind of the young and sensitive boy, as he later recalled in his work.

Gradually, local events became closely connected to events shaping the larger world around him. He moved with his older brother Shawkat, whom he loved and respected, to finish middle school in the city of Zarqa, near Amman, a bustling industrial and military town with Palestinian refugee camps and an active political scene. He then commuted to the capital for his high school education.

Tayseer's life in Zarqa then Amman introduced him to a world beyond the boundaries of his village and its adjacent desert. In 1957, the arrest and imprisonment of his brother Shawkat for his leadership role in Jordan's Free Officers Movement added a new dimension to Tayseer's understanding of the complex issues that his young nation was facing.[9] In his poem "The Absent Eagle," written in 1961, he shared the sadness and pain of the experience, while also acknowledging that despite the pain, the fight continues.

> My eagle! O my eagle!
> your talons sunk deep in the desert,
> bleeding in the sand, you are still fighting.

If your eyes could only glance at me,
they would know how much I have suffered.
My heart,
    my eyes,
all my veins, beg for *water*.
But the water is with the absent eagle,
and the eagle is fighting in the desert.

The newly established Jordanian Ba'ath Party was similar to other parties in the region at the time, actively recruiting in schools and universities.[10] Tayseer joined the party at a great risk.[11] He anticipated participating in what he hoped would lead to the creation of the great nation of which he had always dreamed. He later described the sentiments of the experience through the recollection of the protagonist of his novel, *You as of Today*:

> He quickly accepted the mission of the Party, and nervously prepared for enrollment. The teacher himself would perform the ceremony. He was led by an upperclassman to the secret and exciting event. The teacher was waiting under a large walnut tree. Arabi felt embarrassed by his short pants, which did not seem to fit the dignity of the occasion. He heard the words in praise of him, and other impressive words linking him, with his short pants to the nation as a whole.
>
> He was ready to add more words to the official Party pledge for greater effect, but a sudden sense of respect stopped him from changing the language—the pledge after all was not a game. The teacher and his fellow students congratulated him. He felt the magnitude of what he had secretly gained, and became consumed with a mysterious, wonderful feeling.[12]

Tayseer gradually became frustrated with the party's practices and ideologies that at times conflicted with his straightforward Jordanian culture, rooted in Bedouin honor and keen sense of justice. Further, he was unable to conform to the party's practices that clashed with his vision of a great nation. Disappointed with the performance and corruption of some of its leaders, Tayseer eventually left the Ba'ath Party. This experience was reflected in his novel and some of his poems with brutal honesty void of self-glorification, which is uncommon among Arab writers.[13]

Despite the political struggle in Tayseer's life and the long imprisonment of his brother Shawkat, Tayseer did well in school and received a full scholarship from the Jordanian government to study at the American University of Beirut. With its modern, Westernized lifestyle, Beirut frustrated him, but also helped him better define who he was and what he wanted. During that period, he wrote and published some of his earliest work, including "The Red Indian."[14] This short story is a playful commentary on a nation's search for identity. It starts by relaying the journey of a young Jordanian infatuated with the West—especially with white women and white American cowboys portrayed in the movies his father frequently and enthusiastically took him to watch. Through a series of events, the young man discovers that he is simply another native that Americans see as a mere savage, no different from the Native Americans that he cheered to see slaughtered by the white men in the movies. With the realization that he actually was more like a Native American than a white man, he happily embraced his newly discovered identity and went back home walking proudly with a feather in his hair, like a "Red Indian."

Dismayed with Beirut and its bourgeoisie Western lifestyle at that time, al-Sboul moved to Damascus, which was better suited to him, with its more traditional Arab culture and active literary and political scene. He studied law at the University of Damascus and published prolifically in Syrian and Lebanese newspapers, as well as in prominent literary magazines such as *Al-Thagafah*, *Al-Adab*, and *Al-Adib*. Tayseer's experience in Damascus was rich and turbulent. In addition to his intense political and literary activities, he experienced love and disappointment, and he later met and married his wife, May Al-Yateem.

Tayseer's poems were personal and reflected his own experiences. They were as Ghalib Halasa stated, "able to bring out the genius in the readers."[15] Steeped in cultural references and an array of cultural imagery, practices, norms, and perceptions, his poems expressed his struggle and the struggle of his generation to find love and define their place in life, politics, and the dream of an ever elusive great nation. Tayseer's close friend, Sadiq Abed Al-Haq, maintains that *Desert Sorrows* and all other works by Tayseer reflect events and circumstances Tayseer experienced, internalized, and then wrote about.[16] The poems detailed his moods and disappointments, and his generation's quest for a new way of life that was made impossible by the social restrictions and political turmoil inflicted on the region at the time. That mood was not much different from the struggle Arab youth face today, with the new waves of change sweeping the region.

Tayseer rarely held back in sharing his deepest thoughts and feelings. He wrote about numerous love experiences and heartbreaks. He did not shy from erotic images, but censored himself by avoiding potentially offensive words in the context of his general culture. He exercised great latitude in creating movements and actions that portray the intensity of the experiences. This is best illustrated in his poem "Secrets." The title of the poem and Tayseer's choice to use inanimate objects—a "table" (feminine) and a "chair" (masculine) as substitutes for a man and a woman, and a "stem" and "vase" to describe an intimate encounter—illustrate that despite all of what can be said about Tayseer's openness and rebellion, there were certain social taboos he chose not to break.

The chair reached for the shoulders of the table.
The flower dropped its stem in a vase.
The evening was still.
We listened.
We heard
a whisper in the folds of silence,
and timid steps.
Within us a secret hovered,
fear of the journey.
When she gestured in consent,
my veins pulsed with excitement
seeing the one I had waited for.
The journey starts.
One hand wanders, then rests.
This evening is gentle.
The flower pumps inside the vase.
Silence suffers
the birth pains of movement.

Suddenly, the chair and the table,
their arms entwine.

With the genius of a poet, the skill of a craftsman, and the sensitivity of a lover, Tayseer managed in the same poem to share a profound erotic experience without breaking cultural taboos. Describing his tender reunion with her, he wrote:

The evening is held tightly
in a dress that grips it like a noose.
The world of secrets calls to me, and begs
that I untie it—
suffering, longing, and in pain.
I am in love.
The hissing of weaving over her body
repeats its yearning in my ears,
leads the movements of my hands
in the realm of flexibilities.
Colors in the corner, singing with joy,
a carnival of light,
woven transparent
like a rainbow.

In this poem, and in many others, Tayseer demonstrates his high regard for women. He is never dominant or exploiting, as portrayed in the predominantly Western notion of Arab men's treatment of women. His experience with her is that of an equal, and to her he offered his sincere gratitude for what she had to share.

I pray for you, daughter of light,
so generous this evening,
so unselfish in giving.
How often I have traveled this distance,
my hand reaping its fruits,
my mouth drinking from its flow.
But I am still thirsty, and my blood is hot

with a mad desire to be spilled in it.
So, listen to this banging
as it gushes strong in my arteries,
longs to live inside you.
It is from you
and to you.

Tayseer's belief in equal partnership in love is presented in his poetry and supported by ample examples from his narrative work. In the "Rooster's Cry," a short story he wrote during the same period, he described another intimate experience with the same tender and soft touch of a poet totally in love, equal to his lover.

> They both closed their eyes and allowed the soft warm waters to complete the ritual, a free swing, soaring up high. The blueness of the sea was wild with great white foam; it rushed toward them, shielded them, and washed over them with a tremendous joy. His cries woke the dawn of the primitive earth. A man was united with a woman, and a woman was united with a man, like two halves of a grain of wheat.[17]

Women are ever present in Tayseer's poems—as a friend in whom he confides his sorrows and loneliness, an ex-lover who he brutally scorns, or a young girl crying for help. He moves their plight from the private to the public, as he did in "Desert Sorrows (2)."

The song's
complaint pierced the nights of Mesopotamia,
bearing the night-long yearning of the virgins—
in love, tormented—
filling the nights with pain.
. . . .
Yes, that girl,
a child, alive,
grew up—O God!—
gushed with desire,
stunned by a love she didn't understand,

hungered,

and bent, perplexed.

Complained

of the cruelty of family, the injustice of parents,

and sang *al-'Ataba.*

The song,

when it passed by us,

pierced us through,

and before us, pierced the nights of Mesopotamia.

Tayseer believed that the oppression of women was not an isolated act, but part of a larger, orchestrated political and social oppression that was meant to keep the nation from reaching its dream of glory and greatness. In "What No One Told Us about Scheherazade," Tayseer speaks on behalf of Scheherazade and her suffering. He also asks us to reflect on how different the truth is from the common narrative of Scheherazade's tale that sanctions oppression and invites girls to seek approval and wait for mercy from a strong and generous man, a Shahryar.

My Scheherazade,

my Scheherazade, my friend!

Whatever was said was said.

But you whispered the truth to me:

For a thousand nights,

every night

your only hope was to last through the night.

So when the cock crowed,

announcing to the world the birth of the morning,

you slept with death in your bed.

For a thousand nights,

the light of youth was extinguished from your eyes,

all flavors became the same flavor,

the bitter like the sweet.

After that, it was morning, but was not.

Only the memories of a young girl,

how different from that was Scheherazade!

The deceptive portrait of victory "fixed in the mind of history for centuries" was that "Shahryar pardoned Scheherazade," when he actually was her oppressor. Through the untold story of Scheherazade, Tayseer called attention to a wider problem in his homeland where "[people] entertain [themselves] with your passionate tales / and songs about victory / . . . that never was and never will be" as long as they are under the watchful eyes of mighty and tyrannical Shahryars.

•   •   •

After finishing his studies in Syria, Tayseer returned to Jordan, disappointed with political life and the failing attempts at unity in the region. He stopped writing and became occupied with work and raising a family.[18] He held various government jobs, eventually taking short-term positions in Bahrain and Saudi Arabia. He then returned to Jordan and opened (and closed) a private law practice in Zarqa. Eventually, he accepted a position as a writer, producer, and host of a radio talk show called *With the New Generation*. His warm personality, wide knowledge, and genuine interest made the show a great success. It featured up-and-coming Arab and Jordanian writers and poets. This was the job he held at the time of his suicide.

During the 1967 War, he watched the Israeli airplanes bomb the airport in Jordan and witnessed the confusion and devastation. In *You as of Today* he took readers into the shelters, streets, and a demolished bridge to see, smell, and record people's responses to the war and its aftermath. The novel—which documented not only the war but also the intricate details of the life and the perspectives of Jordanians during that period—won the prestigious Al-Nahar award for best novel and became an instant sensation.

Tayseer also described his reactions to the war in "Elegy of the First Caravan":

Sadness shreds the fabric of my heart,
reaches from my heart
to eternity.

And in describing the battlefield he writes:

Twenty thousand eyeballs
picked out by vultures.
Don't conjure up a false victory.
I am telling you,
believe it:
There was no light there.
The night prevailed.
. . . .
The evening turned dark with the abasement of my people,
and night prevailed.

In his typical demand for the exposure of the truth no matter how
hurtful it could be, he called on Arabs to stop pretending and face their
reality of defeat:

Forget the ranting of ignorant men,
forget the lies of demagogues.
It is here in my eyes:
the wind is heavy with shame
blowing over children and grandchildren,
reaching into time.

Despite the defeat and darkness, Tayseer believed, as he expressed
in his novel and poetry, that there would be a morning following the
dark gloomy night of defeat and that the sacrificed blood would not go
to waste. He predicted that these sacrifices would be "the oil that lights
the minaret."

This, just the first caravan.
So, keep the honor of being the first
a secret in the consciousness of the sand.
One day, when the curtains of night open to dawn,
you will know that our blood
is the oil that lights the minaret.
It will be said that this defeat
mapped for those who came after their pride.

The 1967 War greatly impacted Tayseer. He tried to understand what happened to his nation, and when he failed, he went back to history looking for answers. His novel, like his poems, portrayed with great honesty his thoughts and feelings, describing events and people's reactions to what he saw happen and giving readers access to the minds and hearts of a generation of Jordanians at a critical time in history.

Ghalib Halasa wrote that Tayseer's novel "does not only redefine our daily life in a new light, but also gives us the freedom . . . to recall . . . the freedom to link actual events to all their connections, putting in motion a new dynamic. It trains the mind to move forward in its inquiry to the end."[19] On a technical note, Halasa pointed out that "employing the techniques Tayseer used in his novel made the novel beautiful aesthetically . . . [a beauty that] rested in its freshness, and the power that makes us discover ourselves and rediscover the truths we know but usually choose to ignore."[20]

The novel's influence extended beyond self-discovery discussed by Halasa to influence the field of Arabic literature at large. In his critical essay, Ahmad Majdoubeh considered the novel a "masterpiece," "pioneering," and "creative postmodernist" work that altered the course of the Arabic novel.[21]

Through all the trouble and agony Tayseer faced, he still had loyal friends who loved him, respected him, and valued and appreciated him as a poet and a writer. He frequently argued with them over politics and life, but they were always there for him.

During my visit to Jordan in the summer of 2013, in addition to meeting Tayseer's family, I was fortunate to meet Suliman Al-Azrai, who dedicated a significant portion of his academic career to the study of Tayseer's life and work. I also met some of Tayseer's old friends, including Adi Medanat and Sulima Al-Gawab'a, who still remember him fondly. For them and all his other friends, he wrote "My Return to Tired Comrades":

My solace:
friends who did not crucify Jassas for his betrayal,
they ask for love and they give love—kindness,
they forgive.
We all betray someone.

Through his education and career, Tayseer was politically and socially evolving, but no matter what he learned and wherever he went, he remained a Jordanian Bedouin. This strong sense of identity was first expressed in his short story "The Red Indian," when he discovered that he was more akin to a Native American than a white man. This strong sense of belonging to Jordan is also reflected in his poetry, including his choice of his poetry collection's title, *Desert Sorrows*. The poem "Desert Sorrows (1)" flows from Tayseer's stream of consciousness, with intricate scenes and imagery that reflect his state of spirit and mind. At a moment of yearning and reflection, Tayseer, the Bedouin, and the desert become the agent and the object, the recipient and reciprocator of a series of recollections, intense feelings, and trajectories of the future.

> From time before time,
> in the darkest caves of eternity,
> it stretched through the Arabian Desert,
> flowing like a dream, magic, melancholy,
> like the nights of Scheherazade,
> crossed dune tops,
>> traversed ravines.
> From time before time,
> the grains of sand,
> drank the sorrow in that voice,
> entered it in their folds,
> returned it to me,
> flowing like a dream, magic, melancholy.
> As I breathe in its sorrows,
> the voice in the folds of my chest
> revives my longing for him.
> I see him,
> a Bedouin with hopeless steps mapped in the desert,
> lonely, waiting for traces of dewdrops
> from time before time.
> And yet,
> once that longing awakens in my heart
> for more nearness and touch,

and once the call for confession clamors
in the chambers of my soul,
when I am startled to find
my death in each fleeting moment,
when I know that I am
part of the warmth of the others,
I imagine seeing him again,
a Bedouin with hopeless steps mapped in the desert,
walking, the glare of the sun in his eyes,
the sand promising more sand,
the stretch of the desert—silence,
the torment of departure.

Through language and metaphors, Tayseer imprinted the intangible upon the tangible and infused them together, demonstrating an inseparable relationship between the place and person. To readers familiar with Bedouins and their affinity for the desert, the images are realistic, and the rhythm of the poem, melodious and soul staring, draws listeners into a swirl of emotions that glues the poem together. This and other poems became an iconic representation of the intimate relationship the Bedouins have with the desert. The poem was recited by the prominent Jordanian poet and songwriter Hayder Mahmoud, and became widely distributed through YouTube and social network forums.

In October 1973, war raged again, followed by a series of negotiations and political maneuverings that Tayseer saw as surrender and defeat. According to his wife, the 1973 War and the events that followed were incomprehensible tragedies for Tayseer. He lost hope and felt that he could no longer bring about change. With that, Tayseer lost his desire to live.[22]

On November 15, 1973, in a final act of freewill, Tayseer al-Sboul killed himself. He came back from work at the radio station, asked his wife for a cup of coffee, lay in bed, and before he got the cup of coffee, he shot himself. The news of his death shook the tight-knit Jordanian community and literary scene, which was not accustomed to suicide. The debate over the true reasons behind Tayseer's death raged at the time and continues decades after his departure. People had a difficult time accepting his death. He was young—less than thirty-four years old. He had a wonderful family, with two young children and an intelligent, beautiful wife. He enjoyed the company of close and loyal friends and had a successful and promising career.

Despite this, Tayseer struggled to comprehend his existence; he was conscious of the suffering of his people, trying to make sense of the turmoil affecting his world, and attempting to make a difference. He was constantly looking for his place within his own history, culture, and identity. He was struggling to embrace life and make rational decisions in an irrational world. In his search, Tayseer frequently felt that there was no purpose or explanation at the core of existence and that, in the end, it was as empty as life itself. He consciously took steps toward that end and wrote about that in many of his poems. In "The Journey," he wrote:

> He remembered nothing of the pain of past nights.
> His journey came to an end.
> The promise was on the summit,
> and the summit loomed near.
> A moment,
> the twitch of an eye,
> and there the summit appears.
> He sees
> there is nothing there to see.
> There is nothing there to touch.
> The summit is just empty.

Tayseer was fascinated with great writers who committed suicide. He was especially intrigued by Ernest Hemingway and Vladimir Vladimirovich Mayakvouski.[23] His life had striking similarity with their lives, struggles, and disappointments, and had the same ending too.

Saud Qubailat argues that al-Sboul's life followed a trajectory similar to Mayakvouski's, with the two men sharing similar ideologies, intense love for their nations, and a preoccupation with national affairs. In his essay "That Cloud in the Trousers of Tayseer and Mayakvouski." Qubailat lists similarities between al-Sboul's and Mayakvouski's lives, and he describes the circumstances that led to their deaths and concludes that it was destiny for them to have the same end. In addition to the similar political change in their countries, Qubailat points out a number of other parallels between their lives: the geography of birthplace, their paternal figure's strong attachment to their land and their work on it, their travel for education at an early age and exposure to progressive political thoughts, the care they received from their families, their early and strong involvement in politics and active membership in political parties with socialist/communist ideologies, their dream of a great nation, their disappointment with the political process they thought would bring change and salvation to their people, their tumultuous love relationships expressed in their poetry, their method of suicide with a bullet to the head, and the similarity in the way they chose to say their final words.[24]

Mayakvouski left a short note that ended with a poem:

> As it was told,
> "A trivial thing had ended,"
> the boat of love
> was crushed on the rock of daily life.
> I gave up on life
> failed to express its common sorrows,
> blunders, and faults.
> Be happy![25]

Tayseer left a few verses that completed the eulogy to his father and another short poem without a title:

> My friend, I
> walk in a dream, aware . . .
> wander toward the edge of death.
> A strange prophet I am, who left
> with no destination in mind.
> I will fall. Darkness will no doubt fill my soul,
> a dead prophet, who has yet to reveal a verse.

Both poets gave up on life and refused to see its value or purpose. They both felt that their lives were "trivial" and without a purpose, and that they had failed to say what they wanted to say. Tayseer wrote, "a . . . prophet, who has yet to reveal a verse," and Mayakvouski wrote that he "failed to express [life's] common sorrows, blunders, and faults."

Tayseer's suicide is the most published aspect of his life. In an article on the twelfth anniversary of Tayseer's passing, Osama Fawzi discussed his suicide and listed the names of prominent Arab and international writers who also ended their own lives, suggesting that more attention should be paid to why they did so when they had what seemed to be successful and productive lives.

In his article, Fawzi discloses that despite his diligent research, he was unable to reach a definite answer for al-Sboul's death.[26] Fawzi presents the views of three prominent Arabs who knew Tayseer well. These include "the misunderstanding that he faced from everywhere,"[27] an eye disease that caused him severe headaches and that was expected to eventually lead to complete blindness,[28] and the proposition that "because he reached a state of absolute despair, and felt that he was not able to contribute to social change . . .This caused him [Tayseer] constant concern and mental uncertainty that persisted throughout the last year of his life."[29]

Fawzi speculates that Tayseer may have committed suicide "for philosophical reasons, as he had adopted Sufism during the last part of his life and was frequently asking about life after death. He believed that there was another life that no one knows and that freedom is part of the truth, or the path to it that can be realized by facing death . . . for that reason, he put a gun to his head and went looking for that truth."[30] Suliman Al-Azrai discussed Tayseer's suicide in detail, exploring the physiological, social, and political dimensions of his personality. He concluded that:

> Tayseer was smart, gifted, sensitive, eccentric, patriotic, and revisionary. His idealistic values and brutal honesty caused him many problems. He moved around carrying broad nationalistic dreams, which he tried to materialize through more than one means, but failed. His physiological make up prevented him from off-loading his disappointments, anxiety, and pain, which accumulated through time and became unbearable. He collapsed from the inside and ceased to exist with no option but to place a bullet in his head and take his life.[31]

We translated the work of Tayseer al-Sboul because he was an exceptional poet and writer who wrote with passion and truthfulness about his life and the life of his people. He lived intensely, consumed by a dream to build a great nation, leaving a recorded legacy of human experiences that transcended the boundaries of his private life and circumstanced to speak to the core of feelings, pleasures, and disappointments in each of us. His unique style and the rhythm of his poems are undoubtedly Arabic, while his message is definitely global.

NOTES

1. See a list of authors that praised al-Sboul's work in A. Y. Majdoubeh, "Taysīr al-Subūl's *You As of Today* in a Post-Modernist Context," *Journal of Arabic Literature* 32.3 (2001): 284–301.

2. From a statement by Jeryes Samawi, Jordan's former Minister of Culture, "He [al-Sboul] is a central figure in the Jordanian and Arab literary scene. We cannot discuss Jordanian literature without referring to his creative experience, especially his important novel, *You As of Today*" in http://alsawt.net. See the full article at: http://bit.ly/1i1RHQn.

3. Tayseer al-Sboul, *Ahzan Sahrawiyah* [Desert sorrows] (Beirut, Lebanon: Dar Al-Nahar, 1968). Tayseer al-Sboul, *Tayseer Al-Sboul: Al-A'mal Al-Kamelah* (Amman, Jordan: Dar Al-Azminah, 1998), including poems Tayseer wrote after 1968, was published posthumously by his wife, May Al-Yateem.

4. See the introduction to al-Sboul's complete works by his wife, May Al-Yateem in al-Sboul, *Tayseer Al-Sboul: Al-A'mal Al-Kamelah*, 10. The collection was published posthumously in 1998 and in 2005.

5. Tayseer al-Sboul, *You as of Today*, trans. Nesreen Akhtarkhavari (Amman, Jordan: Jordanian Writers Society, 2012), 33.

6. Tayseer al-Sboul, *Toi, de's aujourd' hui*, trans. Wael Rabadi (Amman, Jordan: Ministry of Culture, 2012).

7. Suliman Al-Azrai, *Al-Kalima wal Rasasa: Derasah fe Hayat wa Athar Al-Adeeb Al-Rahel Tayseer Al-Sboul* [The word and the bullet: a study of the life and work of Tayseer Al-Sboul] (Amman, Jordan: Jordanian Ministry of Culture 2013).

8. *Afkar* 296 (September 2013) included articles about Tayseer al-Sboul by

Majdolen Abu Al-Rub, Suliman Al-Azrai, May Al-Yateem, Ghalib Halasa, Saud Qubailat, Adi Madanat, Rasmi Abu Ali, Nesreen Akhtarkhavari, and Jafar Al-Agellie.

9. The movement started in 1952 by officers in the Jordanian Army to purge the army of British control. King Hussain supported the movement in 1953, but later imprisoned many of its leaders, including Shawkat al-Sboul, based on rumors that they were plotting a coup similar to the one orchestrated by the Free Officers in Egypt. Through a general amnesty by the king in 1962, the officers were freed. Many went back to the army and occupied sensitive positions in the government, including directors of national intelligence and defense.

10. The Ba'ath Party was officially launched in Syria in 1947 during a convention that welcomed interested members from numerous Arab countries including Jordan. Upon their return home, the Jordanian participants formed the first branch of the party in Jordan.

11. Membership in political parties in Jordan was prohibited until 1992, when a legislation that allowed and regulated political parties was instated.

12. al-Sboul, *You as of Today*, 27–28.

13. Ghalib Halasa, "Al-Khorouj min Al-Lo'ba," *Afkar* 269 (September 2013).

14. al-Sboul, *Tayseer Al-Sboul: Al-A'mal Al-Kamelah*, 71–78.

15. Halasa, "Al-Khorouj min Al-Lo'ba," 106.

16. Tayseer's letters to Abdul al-Haq were published in *Al-Najar, Tayseer* (2009). "al-Muntaher al-ladhti matazal taskunu miratahu ahzanana al-kubra, rasae'l Tayseer al-Subul. Guswat al-alam hena yakun mahsoos" [The departed whose mirrors still host our great sorrow, Tayseer al-Sboul letters, the sharpness of pain when it is tangible] (*Al-Nazwa* 48, http://www.nizwa.com/word.php).

17. al-Sboul, *Tayseer Al-Sboul: Al-A'mal Al-Kamelah*, 109.

18. Tayseer was survived by his wife May Al-Yateem, his son Otba, and his daughter Saba. They have been very supportive of the translation of Tayseer's work and keen on having it reach Western readers.

19. Ghalib Halasa, "Al-Khorouj min Al-Lo'ba," 100–106.

20. Ibid.

21. Majdoubeh, "Taysīr," 284–301.

22. al-Sboul, *Tayseer Al-Sboul: Al-A'mal Al-Kamelah*, 12.

23. Ernest Hemingway (1899–1961) and Vladimir Mayakvouski (1893–1930)

both killed themselves with self-inflicted shotgun blasts to the head.

24. Saud Qubailat, "Telka al-Ghaymah fi Serwal Tayseer wa Mayakvouski [That cloud in the trousers of Tayseer and Mayakvouski]," *Al-Hewar Al-Mutamaden* 3791 (2012).

25. Translated to English by Nesreen Akhtarkhavari from an Arabic translation by Rifat Salam in *Ghayma fi Pantaloons wa Qasaid Ukhra* [A cloud in a trouser and other poems] (Cairo: The Egyptian Ministry of Culture, 1998), 9.

26. Osama Fawzi. "Writer's Suicide: On the Occasion of the Twelfth Anniversary of the Suicide of the Jordanian Poet Tayseer al-Sboul, Writer's Suicide a Phenomena that Deserve to be Studied," *Arab Times*, 1985, http://www.arabtimes.com/osama-all/doc35.html.

27. A letter from Fouad al-Takrely to Osama Fawzi dated 24 September 1976 in Fawzi, "Writer's Suicide."

28. A letter from Issa al-Naouri to Osama Fawzi dated 22 February 1976 in Fawzi, "Writer's Suicide."

29. Saleh Soudah in correspondence sent to Osama Fawzi (date unknown) in Fawzi, "Writer's Suicide."

30. Fawzi, "Writer's Suicide."

31. Al-Azrai, *Al-Kalima wal Rasasa*, 74.

Winter

شتاء

أحزان صحراوية (1)

مِن زمان
مِن تجاويف كهوفِ الأزليّه
كان ينسابُ على مدّ الصحارى العربيّة
ليّنا كالحلم سحرياً شَجيّا
كليالي شهرزاد
يتخطى قمم الكثبانِ
يجتاز الوهاد.

من زمان
شربت حسرةَ ذاك الصوتِ
حباتُ الرمال
مزَجَتهُ في حَناياها
أعادته إليّا
ليّناً كالحُلم سِحرياً شَجيّا
فكأني قد تنفستُ شجونه
وكأن الصوتَ في طياتِ صدري
رجّع اليومَ حنينه
فأراه
بدوياً خطّت الصحراءُ لا جدوى خطاه
موحشاً يرقُبُ آثار الطلول
مِن زَمان
غير أني
كلما استيقظ في قلبي اشتياق
لمزيدٍ من تَداني والتصاق
كلما ضَجَ نداءُ البَوح
في أرجاءٍ ذاتي
كلما بُوغتُ أني
أتناهى بانسِراب اللحظاتِ
كلما أحسستُ أني
بعضُ دفءَ الآخرين
خلتُني عُدت أراهُ
بدوياً خطّت الصحراءُ لا جدوى خطاه
سارَ في عينيه وَهجُ الشمسِ

Desert Sorrows (1)

From time before time,
in the darkest caves of eternity,
it stretched through the Arabian Desert,
flowing like a dream, magic, melancholy,
like the nights of Scheherazade,
crossed dune tops,
        traversed ravines.
From time before time,
the grains of sand
drank the sorrow in that voice,
entered it in their folds,
returned it to me,
flowing like a dream, magic, melancholy.
As I breathe in its sorrows,
the voice in the folds of my chest
revives my longing for him.
I see him,
a Bedouin with hopeless steps mapped in the desert,
lonely, waiting for traces of dewdrops,
from time before time.
And yet,
once that longing awakens in my heart
for more nearness and touch,
and once the call for confession clamors
in the chambers of my soul,
when I am startled to find
my death in each fleeting moment,
when I know that I am
part of the warmth of the others,
I imagine seeing him again,
a Bedouin with hopeless steps mapped in the desert,
walking, the glare of the sun in his eyes,

والرملُ وعودٌ برمال
ومدى الصحراءِ صمتٌ
وعذابات ارتحال،
فتغنّى
وسَرى الصوتُ على مدِّ الصحارى العربيّة
مودعاً في الرملِ غصّاتِ أغانيهِ الشجيّة.

the sand promising more sand,
the stretch of the desert—silence,
the torment of departure.
He sang.
His voice stretched through the Arabian Desert,
leaving the sorrow of his songs in the sand.

السؤال

قبل هذا اليوم كان
كان طفلا
ملءُ عينيه سؤال
ولذا غذَّ خُطاه
مسرعاً خلف رؤاه
يستطيب الإرتحال،
وهنا باغَتَهُ الصوتُ وقال:
(حيثُما وجّهت لا "أينَ"
فقف
هذه أرضُ المُحال).
قبل هذا اليوم كان
كان طفلا
وهو طفلًا ما يزال.
ولقد يعبُرُ حيناً
سالكاً أيّ اتجاه،
ولقد يذّكر طيفاً
من قديماتِ رُؤاه
ولقد يضحك أو يبكي
فطفلًا ما يزال
هو يحيا
والذي مات السؤال.

The Question

Before this day was,
he was a child.
>A question filled his eyes.
So he ran hard,
raced after his visions,
>enjoyed his journeys.
Here, a voice surprises him and says:
Wherever you went, you went to no- "where."
>*So, stop!*
This is the land of the impossible.
Before this day was,
he was a child.
He is still a child.
He might journey out at times,
going in whatever direction.
He might remember an image
from his old visions.
He might laugh, or cry.
A child he still is.
The child still lives.
What died is the question.

شتاء لا يرحل

على أُفقنا تَتَمطى الغيوم
تَجُوبُ ببطءٍ تُخوم السماء
وتوشك تهمس أنَّ الشتاء
تنَاهى
وَودَّع أيامَنا
وخلَّف في الأرضِ أحلامَنا
وُعُوداً بِخَصبٍ
ثماراً لحُبٍّ
وَعَاهُ ضمير الثَّرى والمطر.
تناهى الشتاء
تنَاهى الضجر
قريباً يُطل علينا القمر
ينقل فوق التلال خُطاه
ويَسكُبُ في عُمقنا من ضِياه
تَناهى الشتاء
تَناهى الضجر
وأعلمُ أني أحبُّ الربيعَ
وأصبو إليه صُبّوَ اشتهاء
ولكنّ قلبي يُعاني شِتاء
شِتاء،
يلوحُ بلا مَوسم مُنتَظر
أحسُّ الدموع به تَنهمر
وأسمعُ فيه خُواء الرِّياح
ورَجع النُّواح
شِتاءٌ
شِتاء،
يلوحُ بلا مَوسم مُنتَظر
وماذا لو أَن القَمر
تغيَّب عَن أُفقنا أو خَطَر
سَواء
سَواء
فعُمري شِتاء.

Winter Will Not End

On my horizon, clouds stretch out,
drifting into the deep sky,
whispering that winter
is over.
       It said goodbye to our days,
buried our dreams in the ground,
the promises of growth,
the fruits of love.
The soil and the rain understood.
Winter ended.
       Boredom ended.
Soon the moon will appear,
strolling above the hills,
pouring its light on my soul.
Winter has ended.
Boredom has ended.
I know I love the spring.
I long for it with desire.
But my suffering heart, full of winter.
       Winter,
appears at no fixed season.
I feel tears pour out,
hear the howling of the wind,
the echo of weeping.
Winter.
       Winter,
appears here with no fixed season.
What if the moon
left the sky, or disappeared?
All the same.
All the same.
My life is winter.

أشباح الرجال

كان إحساساً عميقاً لا يسمّى
مُبهماً يبعثُ فينا
غَبطةَ نَشوى وأمنا
دافئاً يَحبو على الأعصابِ
يغفو مطمئنًا . . .
تذكرين؟
زائرٌ من غير ميعادٍ أتانا
لم يكن يحمل في الكفّين
تبراً أو جُمانا
يَحملُ النمنمةَ السُّكرى
يَدُعُّ الأكبُد الظمأى حنانا.
تذكرين؟
مَسَح الأحزانَ عنّا
ثم ضاع اليومَ منّا
ضاع منّا.
حَين غَشا أُفقَنا غَيمُ ارتياب
وتلعثمتِ بذُعرٍ واضطراب
أعتَمت عيناكِ من كل بريق
وتبدّت صُورُ الماضي العتيق
تتلوّى خلف أهدابِكِ
أشباح الرجال
وأنا أصرخُ – تكذيباً لعينيّ – (محال)
لحظةً مضنيةُ الصّمت
هَوى نَجمي – تلاشى لزَوال
والمروجُ الخضرُ بالأمس تَعَرّت
واستحالت ليباب
فإذا صدرُكِ اخوى مِن خراب
وإذا أنتِ
كقبرٍ مُتداعٍ تحت أطباق التُراب.

Ghosts of Men

This deep feeling I can't describe,
it is mysterious, invokes
ecstasy and peace.
Warm, it crawls through the nerves,
slumbers serenely . . .
          Remember?
That guest who came unannounced,
who didn't bring gifts of gold or silver,
who carried intoxicated tingling
and deposited tenderness in our thirsty breasts.
          Remember?
He wiped away our sadness.
Today we lost him.
We lost him.
When our horizon darkens with clouds of suspicion,
and I stutter with terror and distrust,
your eyes blur, lose their lust.
The images of the past disappear,
and beneath your eyelashes
          the ghosts of men contort.
I scream, disbelieving what I see. (Impossible!)
A moment of silent agony.
My stars fall—vanish in nothingness.
The green pastures stripped yesterday
lie barren.
Your chest empty, in ruins.
And you,
a grave crumbling under piles of dirt.

لحظات من خشب

أَنا والمذياعُ والليلةُ عيد
والمُغَنّي يمضغُ الفَرحةَ
في مطٍّ بليد
ولُفافاتي استقرَّت
جُثَثاً بين الرماد.
كُنتُ أشتاق لو أن التبغ في صَدري
ذُو طَعمٍ ولو كانَ مَرير.
كُنتُ أشتاقُ لو أنّي
لي بهذا العيد أفراحُ صَغير،
أو لو أني
لي به فجعانُ مأتم
كُنتُ أعلم
أن عيداً بعد عيدٍ بعد عيد
سوف تأتي
ثُم تَمضي
وأنا أحرقُ تَبغاً
ونَفَايا ذكريات
وأنا أنظرُ من شاطِئي
الصخريِّ في نهرِ الحياة.

كُنتُ أعلم
أنني ضيّعت مأساتي وأنّي
مرةً في العمرِ لم أقبض مَسرّه
أنني ما عُدت أعصاباً
وعظماً -صِرتُ فِكره
مَحضَ فكره.

Moments of Wood

The radio and I celebrate tonight,
the singer chewing joy
on a long stretched note,
my cigarettes resting
as corpses among the ashes.
I long for the tobacco in my chest,
to have some taste, even if bitter.
I long for the
festival to bring me a little joy,
or to bring me
the horror of death.
I know
that festival, after festival, after festival
will come
and go,
and I will still be burning tobacco
and scraps of my memories,
watching the river of life
from my rocky shores.

I know
I lost my tragedy, and I
never in life caught hold of happiness.
I am no longer flesh and nerve
and bone—I have become a thought,
a mere thought.

حلولية

كان المساء
نهنهةٌ طريةٌ تنسل في مجاهلِ السماء
وواحداً مَثُلْتُ فوق ضِجعة الخليج
للحظةٍ منسيةٍ بغير ما يقين
تراشقت في خاطري أصداء
كأنَّما نشيج
أنا الحزين أم هي الاشياء؟
خطوتُ خطوتين
أسفتُ أن وَطئتُ فوق مهجِة السكينه
ظننتُ أنني
أعود والزمانَ للوراء
من قبل ألف دورة وقفتُ والمساء
نهنهةٌ طريةٌ تنسلّ في مَجاهل السماء
"عيناي أين كانتا" ؟
غيَّبني السؤال
أنا أكون
لم أكن
وحين لا أكون
من الذي يرى الخليج والصخور والفضاء
لعلها،
لعلها الأشياء
ترى إلى الاشياء

Pantheism

It is evening,
a soft murmur escapes from the mystery of the sky.
Alone, I lift myself up over the slumber of the gulf
in a forgotten moment, without faith.
In my mind echoes clash, riot
like the sound of weeping.
Is it me who is sad? Or are these things sad?
I took two steps,
then I regretted stepping on the heart of serenity.
I thought I
had gone back in time,
back a thousand years. I stood. The evening became
a soft murmur escaped from the mystery of the sky.

     My eyes, where were they?

The question puzzled me.
I was,
I was not.
And when not,
who sees the gulf, the rocks, the sky?
Perhaps,
perhaps these things
see each other.

عودة الشيخ

هوذا شيخ الشتاء
أغلقَ الأفقُ وجاء
هو ذا ينقل في الشارع نَقرات عصاه
قادمٌ يحملُ في سرٍّ إهابه
أدواتٍ مِن فنونِ السِّحره
ريشةٌ تَرسُم أقواساً على عرضِ السماء
وزناداً يُشعلُ البرقَ وغليوناً لتصعيد الغمام
فقفوا
ودَعوا لغو الكلام
واهتفوا
مرحباً، شيخَ الشتاء.

The Return of the Shaykh

Here comes Old Man Winter!
He shut down the horizon and came.
Here he is, moving through the streets, tapping his stick,
approaching, carrying in his bag of tricks
the tools of sorcery—
a feather to draw arcs across the sky,
a torch to ignite the lightning, a pipe to billow out clouds.
So, stop!
       Leave behind your chatter
and cheer.
Welcome, Old Man Winter!

Shaykh, or *Sheikh*, is an honorific title that means "elder" and carries the
meaning "tribal or religious leader." In this poem, it refers to an elder.

Glitter of Temptation

وميض الرغبة

نيسان وحكمه الجدار

ملقىً هُنا في غُرفتي
ووجهكِ البريء يا صديقتي
يلوح عبر وَحدتي
إشراقهُ
حنوّهُ
ينسابُ في أوردتي
يعيدني إلى ضفاف البارحة،

البارحة
[نيسانُ وموسيقى الأعماق
وحنايا مبهمة الأشواق
وجنون اثنين إلى المطلق
قد ضاقت عنه الأمواق

ألقتهُ
لِتيه الاسطورة
ابحرنا نُنشد نجمينا
طوّفنا دنيا من ألقِ
لا تعرفُ بُعداً أو حداً
إبحارُ أبداً إبحار
ويُخّدر فينا الأبصار
واخترنا عفوأ نجمين
وضحكنا ضحكة طفلين
وصممتُ لَدُن حانت نظرة
كانا،

نجمين بعيدينِ]
صديقتي
ملقىً هنا في غرفتي
لربما يحفرُ الزمانُ جبهتي
وربما أحال عمري المضيّعا
صحراءً بلقعا
لكنني
فى عمق سرِ العظمِ في ضميرِ كُلّ جارحه

April and the Wisdom of the Wall

Thrown here into my room,
your innocent face, my friend,
appears to me in my loneliness.
Its brightness,
its softness,
pumps through my arteries,
returns me to the shores of yesterday.

Yesterday:
>   *April and deep music,*
>   *hearts with a mysterious longing,*
>   *two of us swerving toward the absolute.*
>   *My eyes had no space for it,*
> cast it away
>   *into the shadows of a fantasy.*
> *We sailed, seeking our twin stars,*
> *crossed a world of brightness*
> that knows no distance or limit,
> sailing, always sailing,
> with numbed vision.
> We chose two stars at random,
> laughed the laughter of two children,
> *stayed silent till a glimmer appeared*
> *of two*
>   *distant stars.*
My friend,
thrown here into my room,
perhaps time will carve its marks on my forehead,
and turn my wasted life
into a barren desert.
But I,
deep in the mystery of my bones, in the consciousness of every limb,

قطّرتُ نكرى البارحة.
أظلُ يا صديقتي
يا نبعةً سخيّة الحنان
أذكرها ما عادني نيسان.
لكنما
معذرةً صديقتي
وددتُ لو ازوّق الحروف
أهديكها
اغنية مسحورة الطيوف.
حين الخيالُ موثقٌ
على صليب غصتي.
فنحن يا صديقتي
نحن الذين إذ نسير نُطرقُ الجباه
خُطُّ لنا، من قبلُ أن نجيء للحياة
لسنا بفرسان الخيال، إنْ نُثِر نُطاعٌ.
حياتنا، لو تعلمَين، مُرَّة الصراع
من أجل عار لقمةٍ
وسُترةٍ عن العيون
شعارنا ما زال من قرون
(مع الجدار سِرْ
تَكُفَّ قيلةٌ عليك).
ونحن إذ نجوع نصمتُ
لكي تكف شرها العيون.

والبارحة
غَفلتُ يا صديقتي
عن حكمة الجدار،
فمُهجتي
أضحت لحين واله
بحبّ نجم مبعدٍ
يُقال إن الآلهه
خصّته لي رفيق

purify, drop by drop, the memory of yesterday.
I still, my friend,
you wellspring of tenderness!
still remember you when April comes 'round.
But
forgive me, my friend,
I am trying to decorate the alphabet
give it as a gift to you,
a song with magical shadows,
where imagination is tied
to the cross of my sobbing.
We are, my friend,
we are the ones who keep our heads down when we walk.
This was decreed for us before we were born.

We are not the knights of fairy tales,
that when we point we are obeyed.
Our life, you know, is bitter struggle
for the shame of a bite to eat
and a shield from evil eyes.
Our mantra of centuries past remains:
Walk close to the wall and
let no scandal reach you.
If we are yearning, we keep silent
so no eyes will do us harm.

Yesterday,
I forgot the wisdom of the wall.
My heart
found its longing for a while,
in love with a distant star.
They said those goddesses
chose that star as a companion for me,

وكان أنْ أطعتُ ما تلفق الظنون.
وكان يا صديقتي
حلماً قصيراً لاح وانطفأ
وعدتُ للتراب
ممزقاً، مضيعاً
مُشتت اللباب
صديقتي
وأنبأت خُرافةُ النجوم
عن ألفِ سورٍ بيننا
لأن لي شعارٌ
خُلقتُ
كي تَصدق فيَّ
حكمةُ الجدار.

and I obeyed what their suspicions had spun out.
It was, my friend,
a short dream. It appeared and disappeared.
I fell back onto the dust,
dismembered, lost,
with my mind fragmented.
My friend,
the myth of the moon foretold
a thousand walls would fall between us
because I was true to my pledge:
I was created
      to be the one who proves
            the wisdom of the wall.

الحلم

وكنتِ معبّقةً بالبهار
تراخى بهارُكِ
حوّمَ
حطّ
وأنشبَ في عَصبي قسوتهُ.
كأنك حين خطرتِ إليَّ
وطئتِ أديمي
وعانى خُطاكِ البطيئةَ صدري،
وعيناك أثقلتاني وُعود
وفي كلّ وعدٍ
ذؤابةُ نصلٍ يمسُّ الوريد.
قُرابةَ عيني أنتِ
وأبعدُ ما يَعيه مَدى،
عرفتُ: محالٌ عُبوري إليكِ
وغذّ ندائي إليكِ سُدى
كبوتُ عِيّا
رأيتُكِ تنأيْنَ عنّي
وعيناكِ ما زالتا تُومئانِ إليّا
نأيتُ
نأيتِ
تحولتِ أفُقاً بعيداً
وكُنتُ مُسَجّى
وكنتُ وحيدا.
صباحاً خرجتُ
التقيتُ بوجه المدينة
رأيتُ إلى الشمسِ تَضحكُ في الافق
لكن نفسي كانت حزينة
رويداً أسيرُ
ويُطبق ـ فيما اسير ـ عليّ الزّحام.

The Dream

You were dripping with spices:
Your spice breaks loose,
hovers,
lands,
plunges its cruelty into my nerves.
As if when you cross my mind,
you walk on my flesh,
my chest burns with your slow steps,
your eyes fill me with promises,
and with each promise
the edge of your blade slides across my life vein.
You are so close to my eyes,
farther away than distance can reach.
I knew then: It was impossible to reach you.
My call for you was useless.
I fell sick.
I saw you get away from me,
and your eyes still call me.
You went far,
you went far,
became a distant horizon.
I was laid out,
and I was alone.
In the morning, I left.
I saw the face of the city.
I saw the sun smile in the sky.
But my soul was sad.
Now, I walk slowly.
While I am walking, the crowd closes in on me.

احزان صحراوية (2)

العتابا
جَرّحت باللّوم ليلَ الرافِدين
حَملت في الليلِ أشواق العذارى
صبواتٍ تتلوّى
تترعُ الليل عذابا
من متاهات الصحارى
قادِمُ هذا الصدى
أيُّ اصقاع طواها
متعباً جاز المدى
وكبّا
عندَ أعتاب السهارى.
صمت السُّمار، أصخوا
لصدىً يغوي حنيناً
وادكّارا.
يا لهاتيك البُنيّة
طفلةً كانت حيّية
كبُرت، يا مُقلتي فَارت رِغابا
بوغتت بالحبّ، لم تدرِ
تشهّت
وانشت حيرى.
تشكّت
قسوةُ الأهلِ وجَور الوالدين
وتغنّت بالعتابا
والعتابا
حين طافت بنا
جرَّحتنا
جرّحت من قبلُ ليل الرافِدين.

Desert Sorrows (2)

The song's
complaint pierced the nights of Mesopotamia,
bearing the night-long yearning of the virgins—
in love, tormented—
filling the nights with pain.
From the depth of the desert
this echo returns.
What lands it traversed!
Exhausted, crossing distances.
It fell
on the doorstep of the ones still awake.
The party is silent. They listen
to an echo that tempts desire,
memories.
Yes, that girl,
a child, alive,
grew up—O God!—
gushed with desire,
stunned by a love she didn't understand,
hungered,
and bent, perplexed.
Complained
of the cruelty of family, the injustice of parents,
and sang *al-'Ataba*.
The song,
when it passed by us,
pierced us through,
and before us, pierced the nights of Mesopotamia.

Al-'Ataba is a traditional form of Arabic song that chides a lover
through sadness and yearning.

مرحبا

رُغم أن الحبَّ مات
رُغم أنّ الذكريات
لم تعُد شيئاً ثمينا
مالذي نخسر إن نحنُ التقينا
ابتسمنا وانحنينا
وهمسنا:
مرحبا
ومضينا.
ليس يدري ما الذي نضمرهُ
في خافقينا
مرحباً كاذبةً نُسكتُ فيها الناسَ
حتى لا يقال
"آه يا عيني على الأحبابِ
عشّاق الخيال".
وحدَنا نعلم أنّا
افترقنا
واتنتهى ما كانَ مِن حبٍّ قديمٍ
يوم قُلناها مَعَا:
"حبُّنا كان خُرافة".
نحن كفّناه بالصمتِ
ضَنَنَّا أن نُريق الأَدمُعا
وافترقنا
غير أنَّ الأخرين
أعيُن مفتوحةٌ دوماً علينا
فَدَعينا
نَمنعُ الألسُنِ أن تمضُغَنا،
وإذا نحن التقينا
ابتسمنا
وانحنيا
وهمسنا:
مرحبا

Hello

Even though love died,
even though the memories
are no longer precious,
what would we lose if we met,
greeted each other and smiled,
whispered:
Hello
and then left?
No one knows what we hold
in our hearts.
A fake *hello* to silence them,
so they won't say:
"Pity the poor lovers,
            those hopeless lovers."
Only we know
we separated,
and the love we had ended.
When together, we said:
"Our love was an illusion."
We shrouded it with silence.

We blinked back our tears
and separated.
But the others,
eyes open, are always watching us.
So let us
have no gossip.
Whenever we meet,
smile,
bow,
and whisper:
            Hello.

العقد المفروط

وقالت: "في أطلال القصر المهجور، لمحت عقداً مفروطاً، رفعتُ منه خرزة زرقاء
وأحسست أنه كان لي في يوم ما".

1

اللقاء

الغريبان استفاقا
وُلدا ذاك المساء
فجأةً
والوجه للوجه:
لقاء.
المسا يمطر حباً وأسى
والأسى حلوٌ ومرُّ
ورُؤى مكدودةِ الخطو تمرُّ.
"خرزةٌ زرقاء أهدتك الخلود
صحوةٌ في عيد ميلادٍ جديد
أيُّ عقدٍ فُرطت حباته
بين يديكِ
في طلول القمر أغرى ناظريكِ
فانحنيتِ
بنتَ عشرين، استقمتِ
وعصورٌ قبل روما
هرمتْ في مُقلتيكِ"

2

نعيبُ البوم

المساءْ
رعشةُ العرق بتوقٍ للبكاءْ
غصةٌ في القلب،
أثقال رصاص في الضمير
وتلوّ يائسٍ خوف المصير

32 •

The Broken Necklace

She said: "At the ruins of the abandoned palace, I noticed a broken necklace, picked up a blue bead, and felt as if it once had been mine."

1

THE MEETING

The two strangers woke up
and were born again that evening.
Suddenly,
   face to face:
      a meeting.
The evening rains love and sorrow.
The sorrow is sweet and bitter.
Visions pass by with weary steps.
A blue bead bestows eternal life upon you.
You woke up. You were born again.
The necklace scattered its beads
in your hands
when the moon rose, tempted your eyes,
so you bent—
a girl of twenty years—when you stood straight,
ages before Rome,
grew old in your eyes.

2

WHOPPING OF THE OWL

The evening,
the tremble of my arteries longing to weep,
the shock in my heart,
the weight of lead on my conscience,
a desperate twist, the fear of my destiny.

فاسمعيها يا صديقة.
"خرزةٌ زرقاء لا تعطي حقيقة،
وكلانا رحلةٌ مبهمة الأبعاد
لا تؤدّي لمرفأ
فإذا طيفٌ من التاريخ أومأ
لامسَ القلب وأغرى بخلود
أو تباشير لميلادٍ جديد
صدقيني – أنت عيني -
إنه ومض الغوايات الكذوبِ".

3
طريق العودة

المساء أغنيةٌ أسيانةٌ ترتادُ قلبي
والمصابيح ترشُّ الضَوء محزوناً بدربى
اى "باندورا" من المجهولِ جاءَت
عبرت لاتفتدينى
تركَتْني
حائراً ما بين ظني ويقيني
فجاةً، والوجه للوجه، لقاء
فجأة لا شيء حولي
غير ظلّي
يتهادى موحشَ الوجه بدربي
والمساء أغنيةٌ أسيانةٌ ترتاد قلبي.

Listen to them, my dear.
A blue bead cannot tell the truth.
We both are on a mysterious journey
that ends in no harbor.
So if a beam of light out of history signals to us,
touches our hearts, tempts us with immortality
or promises of a new birth,
believe me—you are my eyes—
it is the evil glitter of temptation.

3
THE WAY BACK

The evening is a desperate song that pierces my heart, • 35
the lanterns scatter a sad light on my path.
Pandora came out of nowhere,
moved through, but didn't set me free.
She left me
perplexed between my doubts and my certitude.
Suddenly, face to face: a meeting
Suddenly, nothing was there
except my shadow,
stumbling, a lonely face on the path.
The evening is a desperate song that pierces my heart.

شهوة التراب

"قال آدم: هذه الآن عظمٌ من عظامي ولحمٌ من لحمي، هذه تدعى امرأة
لأنها من امريءٍ أُخذت، لذلك يترك الرجل أباه وأمه ويلتصق بامرأته
يكونان جسداً واحداً." —الاصحاح الثاني: سفر التكوين

هنا معي
يا ضلعي المقدود بين أضلعي
مفقودتي
كنا نجوس رِقَّةً
صدى لوقع رِفَّة
تهويمةً في خاطرِ الاشياء،
أنفاسُنا
أفكارُنا
أبرأ من سكينةِ الاشياءِ
في مطلقِ العراء

هنا معي
هنا معي
يا ضلعي المقدود بين أضلعي
تأتيني
عيناكِ تَندى لهفةً شهيّة السؤال
مَدى أحاسيسي إليكِ فَأسألي
ما لم يَطُف ببال
وتسألين
تسألين بينما
تموجُ في عينيكِ وقعُ رِقّةٍ
صدى انفلات رِفّة
نجوس في سكينة الاشياء
ثانيةً ننسل عائدينَ
نمجِّد الإله في عُذرية العراء
لكننا

Desire of Dust

> And Adam said, "This is now bone of my bones, and flesh of
> my flesh: she shall be called Woman, because she was taken
> out of Man." Therefore, shall a man leave his father and his
> mother, and shall cleave unto his wife: and they shall be one
> flesh. —Genesis 2:23–24

Here with me,
you, my rib carved from my ribs,
my lost one,
we searched for a gentle trembling,
the echo of the sound of a gentle trembling,
a gasp in the mind of things—
our breath,
our thoughts,
more honest than the silence,
utterly naked.
Here with me,
here with me,
my rib, wedged back among my ribs,
you come,
your eyes dripping with desire, with a teasing question:
how much I love you. A question that
never crossed my mind.
You ask,
you ask while
your eyes roll with the ripple of the soft trembling.
The echo of a fleeting soft trembling
travels into tranquility.
Again we sneak back, return,
glorifying God in the purity of our bareness.
But we are.

-ما أوغل الحنيُن-ها هُنا
وجهاُ لوجٍ ها هُنا
من أجل عينيكِ أحبُّ سقطتي
أحب أرضي الترابَ هذه
وخبزي المجبولَ بالعناء
أرضي التي ورثتُها
من شهوة السؤال في عينيك للمحرّم،
ملعونةً أحبها
يدفقُ حباً قلبُها
أغنيةً لا تنتهي
لا تنتهي

هنا معي
يا ضلعي الأحبُّ بين أضلعي.

How deep is our yearning here!
Face to face, right here,
for the sake of your eyes, I love my sinning.
I love this soil, this dust,
my bread, kneaded with such labor,
the land that I inherited
from the desire in your eyes for the forbidden.
Damn! I love her,
and her heart gushes with love,
an endless song.
          Endless
here with me,
my rib, the most beloved of my ribs.

ملاح

ربما غيري ملاحونَ طافوا كل بحرٍ
قهروا الأمواج والأنواء ليلاً إثر ليلٍ
وأذلوا كل هولٍ
ثم عادوا مِلءَ أيديهم لآلي
ربما ...
لكنني وحدي ولا ملاح غيري.
مَن رمى في بحر عَينيك شراعَه
ضاعَ في عينيك-
لم يخشَ ضياعه
وليكن أني بَدّدت بتطوافيَ عُمري
بينما الشطآنُ تدعوني وتُغري
أن أعود
كنت أدري
رحلةٌ أمعنُ فيها خلفَ سرٍّ
هو في أعماق عينيك ولن يصطاد هذا السرَّغيري.

The Mariner

Perhaps, other mariners sailed on every sea,
conquered waves and death, night after night,
slew every monster,
then returned with fists full of jewels.
Perhaps . . .
But I alone, and no other mariner,
threw my sails into the sea of your eyes.
I was lost in your eyes
and did not fear being lost.
Let it be. I wasted my life wandering.
All the while, the shores called, tempting me
to return.
But I knew
I had begun a journey, to find the secret
in the depth of your eyes. No one will reach it but I.

عصفوره قلبي

عصفورةَ قلبي يا حلوة
يا لون ونكهة أيامي
ضجرٌ في لحمي وعظامي
مذ بَعُدت عينيكِ عن عيني
ضجرُ ضجرُ ضجرُ مضنٍ
ولدُنٌ يتطافر بي نَزَقي
وأحسُ اللحظة من فرقي
تَتطاول تطغى كالأبد.
أشقى وأصيح بها: هيا
قلبي مُنحدَرُ فانزلقي
ودعيني يأكلني قلقي
لا بد ستظهر في الأفق
عصفورة قلبي تأتيني
بجناح حانٍ تحضُنني
وسأسمع همهمة الزمنِ
تَنجاب بعيداً عن أذني
تنجاب
بعيداً
عن أذني.
عصفورة قلبي يا حلوة
مُدّي أغنيةً تَوّاقه
مِن آخر منفاك النائي
تَتسلّق تيه الأجواءِ
(عصفوري، مثلَك مشتاقة
يا لون ونكهة أيامي
وبلحمي ضجرُ وعظامي
حتى تلقاني
عصفوري).
طوفي كل الدنيا دوري
أرجاء الكون المعمورِ
تتناهى يوماً غربتنا
يوما سيكون بميسوري.

Sparrow of my Heart

Sweet sparrow of my heart!
You, color and flavor of my days!
Boredom has lived in my flesh and bone
since your eyes fled so far from my eyes.
Boredom, boredom, exhausting boredom.
When weariness overcomes me,
I feel the moment of my terror
will stretch out to eternity.
Miserable, I cry out to her: "Come!
My heart is falling down. Come fall with me!"
Leave me, then. Let my suspicions devour me.
Surely, she will appear on the horizon,
the sparrow of my heart will come to me,
embrace me with loving wings,
so I will hear the droning of time
being lifted far from my ear,
lifted
far
from my ear.
Sweet sparrow of my heart,
send me a yearning song
from your exile far away,
fill the emptiness of my horizon.
My sparrow, like you, I am longing.
You, the color and flavor of my days!
Boredom lies in my flesh and bone,
until we meet again,
my sparrow.

Travel the world, visit
the corners of the known universe.
Our journey will end one day.

إذ أهتف:

-     عصفورةَ قلبي

أن أسمع صوتك:

-     عصفوري

One day,
when I call:
      "O sparrow of my heart!"
I will hear your voice say:
      "My sparrow!"

الاسرار

مِقعدٌ هـمَّ بكتفيَّ منضدة
وردةٌ ألقَت بساقٍ في الإناء.
ساكنٌ هذا المساء
وأصَحنا
فَسمِعنا
في حنايا الصمت همَسا
وخطىً مُرتعدة.
طافَ فينا خِلسةً
هاجِسٌ مِن سَفَر
حيَن أومأت رضىً
هاجَ أعراقُ المكانِ
رؤيةُ المُنتَظر.
تبدأُ الرحلة، كفٌّ
تَتقرّى ثم تَغفو
ناعمٌ هذا المساء.
تخفقُ الوردةُ في جوفِ الإناء
فإذا الصمتُ يُعاني
من مَخاض الحركة
وإذا المقعد والمنضدة
أذرعٌ مشتبكة.
ضيِّقٌ هذا المساء
برداءٍ ضمَّهُ كالشبكة.
عالَمُ الأسرارِ يدعوني ويَضرعُ
كي أحُلَّه
إنه مُضنىً وتواقٌ وموجعُ
وأنا جِدّ مولَّه
وهسيسُ النسجِ فوقَ الجسدِ
ردٌ في سَمعي حنينه
قادَ نقلاتِ يدي
في مجالاتِ اللُّيونة.
هي ذي الألوانُ في الركنِ تُغنّي بفرحٍ
مهرجانٌ من طيوفِ

Secrets

The chair reached for the shoulders of the table.
The flower dropped its stem in a vase.
The evening was still.
We listened.
We heard
a whisper in the folds of silence,
and timid steps.
Within us a secret hovered,
fear of the journey.
When she gestured in consent,
my veins pulsed with excitement
seeing the one I had waited for.
The journey starts.
One hand wanders, then rests.
This evening is gentle.
The flower pumps inside the vase.
Silence suffers
the birth pains of movement.
Suddenly, the chair and the table,
their arms entwine.
The evening is held tightly
in a dress that grips it like a noose.
The world of secrets calls to me, and begs
that I untie it—
suffering, longing, and in pain.
I am in love.
The hissing of weaving over her body
repeats its yearning in my ears,
leads the movements of my hands
in the realm of flexibilities.
Colors in the corner, singing with joy,
a carnival of light,

صاغها النّسجُ الشَّفوفِ
مثلما قوسُ قُزح
وأُصلّي لكِ يا بنت الضياء
مُغدِقٌ هذا المساء
وسخيٌّ بالعطاء.
هذه الأمداءُ كم سافرتُ فيها
قَطفَت كفّي جناها
واستقَى منها فَمي
غير أني بعدُ ظمآنٌ وتجتاح دمي
رغبةٌ هوجاءُ أن يَهْرق فيها،
فاسمعي هذا الدَوي
إنه يهدر في العرق قوي
إنه يشتاقُ أن يسكنَ فيكِ
إنه منكِ

إليكِ.

woven transparent
like a rainbow.
I pray for you, daughter of light,
so generous this evening,
so unselfish in giving.
How often I have traveled this distance,
my hand reaping its fruits,
my mouth drinking from its flow.
But I am still thirsty, and my blood is hot
with a mad desire to be spilled in it.
So, listen to this banging
as it gushes strong in my arteries,
longs to live inside you.
It is from you

and to you.

ثلاث اغنيات للضياع

1

ظلالم ...

عيناكِ ظلام
عينايَ ظلام
عبثٌ أن نَصنع ضحكتنا
ونحاولُ نَرسُمُ بسمَتنا
فَوق الشفتين
ما جدوى -ما جدوى البَسْمَة؟
والقلبُ تُغلّفُهُ الظُلمة
مهما لفّقنا وَحذَقنا
لابد ستُفجعنا الأيّام
إذ تجلو زيف حكايانا
صَدئين سيظهر قَلبانا
عيناكِ ظلام.

2

لحظة وداع ...

تدرينَ
فلسنا كالعشاق
يبكون إذا ما أَن فراق
تدرينَ
وأُدري قِصتنا
جَمَعتنا الصدفةُ ذات مساء
الوحشةُ تفرشُ صدرينا
والخيبةُ تكسو وجهينا
ثَرثَرنا الليلَ
تَواعدنا
وكذا عُدنا فتلاقينا
والآنَ سئمتِ حكاياتي
كلٌّ مِنا سئم الآخَرَ

Three Songs for Absences

1

DARKNESS ...

Your eyes are darkness.
My eyes are darkness.
It is useless to laugh
or try to draw a smile
over our lips.
Why? What use is a smile?
Hearts covered in darkness.
No matter how much we scheme and plot,
time will make us mourn one day,
when the falseness of our tale comes clear,
and our rusted hearts appear.
Your eyes are darkness.

2

GOODBYE ...

You know,
we are not the kind of lovers
who cry when it's time to separate.
You know our story,
and I know our story.
Coincidence brought us together one evening.
Loneliness flowed over our breasts.
Disappointment shadowed our faces.
We chatted through the night,
            made promises,
returned and met again.
Now, you're bored with my stories,
each bored with the other.

فلنبحث عن لهوٍ آخَر
لن نَسفح أدمُعَنا لفراق
ما كنا يوماً كالعشاق.

وحيد ...

الليلُ أغانٍ تَنتحبُ‌أشواقٌ تهدأ، تضطربُ
تتضوَّر روحي فأُنادي:
لو أَنت تمهَّلت الليلة
لو صدُرك يحضُنني الليلة
كُنا ثَرثَرنا وكذَبنا
وزَعَمنا خيط العتم شُعاع
لو أنَّك...
لكن واأسفا
كلٌّ مِنا قال: وداع.

So, let's find other amusements.
We won't shed tears when we part.
We never were like lovers.

   3
ALONE . . .

The night, songs weeping,
yearning recedes, then erupts again
and torments my soul. I call out:
If you had waited for me tonight,
if your breasts had held me tonight,
we would have chatted and lied,
        pretended that the thread of darkness was a ray of light.   • 53
If you had waited . . .
       Too bad. Instead,
each of us said goodbye.

كلمات ثقيلة

1

دمعتان
طفَتا فوق دخان
وعلى رأس لساني
صَبّتا طعم الأَلق
عندها أحسست قلبي
كنسيجٍ من حريرٍ يَحترق.

2

باسم ماذا؟
ابرُ الحزنٍ على عينيكِ تَنْثَالَ رَذاذا
عمَّدوا في كأس سمّ
عظمك الصافي وعظمي
باسم مَاذا؟
نحنُ جسرٌ للكوابيسِ الثقيلة
تَرعدُ الأجيال فينا
ونعاني الموت غيلة.

3

اعذريني
أنا لم أدفن جبيني
بعمامة
لا ولم يُنحَر يقيني
تحت كرسيّ اعتراف،
غير أني
لي طقوسي وصلاتي
عندما تنزفُ روحي
في حنايا رعشاتي
اعذريني. فالخطيئة
إن تمسّيها استحالت
طفلة مشفقة القلب بريئة.

Unbearable Words

1

Two teardrops
floated behind the smoke,
touched the tip of my tongue,
poured out the meaning of brightness.
Then, I felt my heart
burn like silk cloth.

2

In whose name?
The needles of sadness fall on your eyes like raindrops.
In a chalice of poison they baptize
your pure bones and mine.
In whose name?
We are bridges to unbearable nightmares,
generations storm within us,
and we suffer a sudden death.

3

Forgive me,
I did not bury my forehead
in a turban.
No, and my conscience was not sacrificed
in a confession booth.
But I
have my rituals and prayers,
when my soul bleeds
in the depths of my trembling.
Forgive me . . . but sin,
when touched, turns into
a child, innocent, with a heart full of pity.

4

وتقذف الأمواج بي

وزورقي صغير

مولهٌ برغبةِ الإبحار فوق الأفق،

بوثبةٍ يهمّ أن يطير

مغامراً

وينثني إلى المياهِ حائراً

فموجةٌ تشيله

وموجةٌ تحطمه

رُبّانه يصيح:

(أنا أحبُّ أن أموت بارتعاش المطلق).

يَرتجّ عظمُ زورقي

يَنحلُّ في أغنيةٍ

منسيةٍ

هناك . . .

خلف الشفق.

5

وأبعدُ ـ أبعدُ من كل ما قيل ـ

ما لا يقال

فَلِصقُ ضَميري تظلّ حروفُ

حروفٌ ثِقال

أشلُّ عليها وليسَ تبوحُ

وتفعْم صدري بطعم المحال

لماذا؟

لدُن طَفرتْ دمعتان

رأيتُ بعينيكِ لون دخان

وأحسستُ ما لست أدري

وغُفران عينيكِ

من اجل هذا الذي

لا يقال

تَسّاقطُ، تهمي

دموعُ الرجال.

4

The waves toss me.
My boat is small,
mad with desire to travel beyond the horizon.
With a jump, it tries to fly.
Wild,
it crashes in the water, drifting.
A wave lifts it,
and a wave pulls it down.
The captain cries:
I want to die trembling with the absolute.
The bones of my boat writhe,
break into song,
now forgotten
there . . .
behind the twilight.

5

More—more than all that was said—
was what can't be said,
what remained glued to my consciousness: my alphabet
of unbearable letters.
I juggle them, but they never speak.
They fill my heart with the taste of the impossible.
Why?
When two tears dropped,
I saw your eyes behind the color of smoke.
I felt what I couldn't comprehend.
The forgiveness of your eyes
for that which
can't be said
let loose—undammed—
the tears of all men.

لو. . .

عذاباتُ عمري
وبَوحي إليك بما لا يباح
وغضبةٌ كُبرى
تغالبُ فيَّ دُعاء انطِراح.
يلحّ عليّ
ويصرخُ أنّي
سأبقى وحيداً
أُصالبُ ظنّي
يجفّف روحي لهاثُ التمنّي.
لو أنكِ يوماً شففتِ شففتِ شففتِ
وحُرّكَ فيكِ جمودُ الصنم،
لو أنك أحسست طعم التّناهي
فأحسست معنى صفاء النغم.
لو أنكِ -لو
لبلغت الألوهةَ
إذ فضَّ قلبَكِ سرُّ الألم.
وما زلتُ أسعى
وأشقى
أحاول قبض المُحال
وأعنو
فينحلّ فيَّ الكَلال،
يلفّ عروقي كالأخطبوط وأنتِ هناك
تحبين أن يشتهيكِ الرجال
وعيناكِ وحشيّتانِ تَرودان
أبعد مما يلبّي الرجال
كأنهما تحملان رؤاكِ
جياع العروقِ لأدغالِ غابٍ
رؤاكِ!
تُرى وُلدتِ في الكهوف؟
تُرى رضعتِ من لِبان الذئاب؟
فأفرخ فيكِ نداءُ الأمومةِ
هذا الحنينُ لضربٍ ناب.

If . . .

This agony
confessing to you of what can't be said,
this colossal anger,
resisting an inner call to fall.
It persists,
        screams that I
will remain alone
        growing my suspicions.
My soul dries up from the panting of hope.
If one day you turned pure, pure, pure,
and within you the stiffness of idols moved,
if you knew the taste of nothingness,
you might feel the purity of this song.
If you . . . if
        you could have become God,
if your heart had uncovered the mystery of pain.
I am still searching,
suffering,
        trying to catch the impossible.
This agony,
        this tiredness within me dissolves,
wraps around my veins like an octopus—
and you there,
you love to be wanted by men,
but your eyes are wild and wander
beyond that, beyond what men desire,
and they carry your dreams, those eyes.
Hungry veins for the wilderness,
your dreams!
Were you born in a cave?
Were you suckled on the milk of she-wolves?

عذاباتُ عمري
تحدٍّ، عناءٌ، وقبضُ سراب
ينابيعُ حبٍّ تجفُّ سُدى
وظمأى إلى الدم تَهوي الذئاب.

Is that how the wailing of motherhood grew within you,
a yearning to clench your teeth?

This agony—
fighting, struggling, holding on to a mirage:
The springs of love run dry,
thirsty for the blood wolves desire.

Fighting in the Desert

صراع في صحراء

النسر الغائب

إلى أخي شوكت

يا نسري، آه يا نسري
يا نسراً غاصت في الصحراء مخالبه
يجرحها الرملُ، غالبه
عَرِيتَ عُروقك يا نسري
وكُسِرت جَناحك يا نسري
ومفاصلُ عظمكَ ما وهَنت
أواهٍ يا رفضَ الكِبرِ
لو أُغنيّة
تختصر الآفاق وتمضي
ترِدُ الصحراء المنسيّة
وتهلُّ عليك بأشواقي
تَنصبُ بعينيك تحيّة،
تُنبيك بأنّا ما زلنا
نتشوّفُ نسراً خلّانا
في ذاتِ مساء
لَم يُنكرنا
كنا عطشى – طارَ يجيء بجرعة ماء
طارَ وتاه على الصحراء.
يا نسري، آه يا نسري
في أسرِك مثلي في أسري
لو أغنيّة
عَبر الأبعاد المرميّة
تأتيك تقولُ: بعادك طال
لكن هيهات
يَبِست في حلقي الكلمات
لو نظرةُ عين منكَ تراني
سترى كم صرتُ أعاني
قلبي
عيني

The Absent Eagle

To my brother Shawkat

My eagle! O my eagle!
Your talons sunk deep in the desert,
bleeding in the sand, you are still fighting.
You tore out your veins, my eagle,
broke your wings, my eagle.
The joints of your bones didn't surrender,
you were the pride of resistance.
If only my song
could pass over the horizon,
into the forgotten desert,
carry my longing to you,
pour a greeting into your eyes,
tell you that we still
yearn for the eagle that left us
one evening,
who didn't betray us.
We were thirsty. He went to find a drink of water.
He flew away, lost in the desert.
My eagle, my eagle,
in your prison, you are like me in my prison.
If my song could only
        reach across the distance,
tell you that your absence is long.
O God!
        The words are dry in my throat.
If your eyes could only glance at me,
they would know how much I have suffered.
My heart,
        my eyes,

كل عروقي، تصرخ (ماء)
والماء مع النسر الغائب
والنسر يغالبُ في الصحراء.

all my veins, beg for *water*.
But the water is with the absent eagle,
and the eagle is fighting in the desert.

Shawkat al-Sboul was imprisoned in Jordan for his leadership role in the "Free Officers
Movement" that called for Jordan's independence from Great Britain.

العجاج

مُدلجاً أَسلَم للرِيبة قلبه
مُمعنا خلفَ يقينٍ مُدَّعى
ضيّعٍ ربُّه.
كنتُ امضي
ارفع الساق أحث الخَطو لكن
عبثاً تعبر ساقٌ دون ارض.
ماثلًا في حدقةِ التسآل شاهدتُ
قطاراً من سنين
يتعدى حاملًا ما لست أدري
لسواي
ورؤاي
ضجرٌ خدّدت الريح جبينه
سطرت فيه أحاجيّ
كحّلتُه بذريراتِ عجاجٍ.
ايَ وهمٍ
جمّد التّاريخَ في عروقي وعرى
للرياح الهوج نهرا
تسبحُ الاجيال في خفقتهِ
وهـي لا تسأل إن كانت
ستلقى مستقرًّا.
أي وهمٍ كان
تضليلٌ وحَيْره
خلجةٌ من دونِ أعصابٍ
وخفقٌ في الرماد
وأحاجي
تتهادى في شرايينى طوفان عجاجٍ
حين ساومت على الله نداءَه:
(عد إلى الصمتِ فرحمُ الصمتِ مأوى
لعيونٍ حدّقت من دون جدوى).
وترددتُ
وكدتُ
حينما انشقَّ ضباب التيه فجرا

Dust

Walking the night, his heart succumbed to his suspicions
while pursuing its pretended certitude.
He lost his God.
I used to walk,
put one foot in front of the other, hurry on, but
it's absurd to step forward without ground to step on.
I stood there, my eyes questioning. I saw
a train once, many years ago,
passing by, carrying something—I don't know what—
for someone else.
My vision:
boredom, its forehead scared by a wind
that wrote riddles on it,
lined its eyes with black dust.
Such an illusion!
It froze history in my veins, tore them out to make
a riverbed for the tempestuous wind.
Generations swam in its flow
and never asked if it
would ever find an ending.
What an illusion it was!
Lies and confusion,
a twitch with no nerves,
a heartbeat under the ashes.
Those quarrels
moved through my veins like a sandstorm.
I bargained with God for this. He said:
Go back to silence. The womb of silence is the only refuge
for eyes that stare out aimlessly.
I hesitated
and almost did it.
But the clouds of oblivion opened into dawn

ورَوت عيناكِ في رفّةِ نظره
المكانيْن التي حيرّت المصلوب حَيره
حدثتني
(قطرة الماء التي تنأى إلى الشاطيء
لا تفتح بحرا)
عبثاً تَشهق تَهوي
في حضيض الأرض سرّا
ويظل البحر هدّاراً بإذن
الأبدية.
أبداً يعبرني هذا القطار
حاملًا لي
شجناً -مجداً
رعيلًا من صغار
يَرِثون الأرض والتاريخ من بَعدُ
ولا إدلاج. ولا وَهم غُبار.

when her eyes blinked and watered,
the two spots that had spun my crucified self into wonderment.
She told me:
A drop of water that separates on the shore
cannot form an ocean.
Hopeless, I gasped, dropped
into the secret depths of the earth.
The sea continued to rage, with the blessings of
eternity.
Forever, this train will pass by me,
bring me
            anguish, glory,
and crowds of children
who will inherit earth and history after that:
no night journeys, no illusions made of dust.

من مُغترب

1

صديقتي
تحيةٌ مِن متعبٍ حزين
تحيةٌ تَرعش بالحنين
لَمسةٍ
لكلمتي عَزاء

صديقتي
في المُنتأى أُغالب العَياء
أنسج في الصباحِ من ذكراك أُمنيّه
أحلُمُ بالمَعَادِ
إذ يضمّنا لقاء
أروّعُ من توحُّدي سَحابةَ النهار
لكنَّما يُدركني المساء
إذ تَخرُج الأحزان في مَواكبٍ
مَواكب
نحيلةً
شاحبةً
هَشيمةَ المَناكبِ
تُحاصر الدروب
وتَعْرفُ الغريب
لتستقي من عينيه بَقيةَ الرُّواء
أخافُ يا صديقتي من أوبةِ المساء
غُيومه تَعبُرُني
مُثقلةً بالنشيج
مواكبُ الأحزانِ فيه تملأ الدروب
تحاصر الغَريب
واحسرةَ الغريب.

2

صديقتي
وَجَدَّفُوا علَي
ولوَّثَّت شفاهم آخر ما لدي

From a Sojourner

1

My friend,
my greeting—I am tired, sad—
my greeting trembles with yearning
for a touch,
           for a couple of words of comfort.
My friend,
in my loneliness, I fight exhaustion,
weave hope from your memory at dawn,
dream of the promised day,
           when we will be united by an embrace.
I hide from my loneliness under the cover of day,
but evenings catch up with me,
and an army of sadness marches out in a parade.
           A parade,
thin,
gloomy,
ragged,
lays siege to the streets,
recognizes a stranger,
slurps its fill from his eyes.
I fear, my friend, the dawning of night.
Its clouds pass through me
           full of silent screaming.
Its parade of sadness fills the roads,
seizes the stranger.
How sad is the stranger.

2

My love,
they cursed me.
Their lips soiled the last thing I had,

براءتي
وخيبةَ المَسار
أَللذبابِ – للذبابِ مُنتهى المطاف
يَقتاتُ ذَوْبَ مُهجتي
وتسألين لِمْ أنا حَزين؟
مَعذرةً -فأنت تَسألين
قدّيسة لم تعرف الذباب
في وحشة اغتراب.

3
صديقتي
كل العيون ها هنا حزينه
فالحزن قد غزا المدينه
جنودُهُ الأَقزام قد تسلّقوا البيوت
وحطَّ في آفاقنا سُكوت
تشِي الوجوه ها هنا
بأننا نُشفقي. صديقتي
يَقتاتُنا السأم
بِرقّةٍ ودونما أَلم.

my innocence.
How disappointing is this journey
to flies. Does the journey end with the flies?
They feed on my melting heart,
and you ask, why I am sad?
   Excuse me, you ask.
You, a saint who finds no flies
or loneliness on your journey.

  3
My friend,
all eyes here are sad.
Sadness invaded the city.
Its midget soldiers climbed into our homes.
Silence spreads among us.
Faces speak without words.
We are pitiful, my friend.
Boredom consumes us
softly, without pain.

قطعة قلب للبراءة

تخنقني أصابع الندم
تجتثّني، تُحيلني شريحةً من الألم،
لأنني بريء
وفوق ما تحمله إرادتي
أصحّ:
أكون قد صلبتُ إخوتي
أحبّتي
أضرعُ: يا ايزيس، يا ايزيس
يا مَن فضضتِ أرضَنا
فتحتِ عن عَطائها الحبيس،
لو جُدتِ لي بحفنتي دُموع
غسلتِ لي خطيئتي
حملتِ عن ضميري المعذب
آلامَه وحَماةَ التدنيس
لو جُدتِ يا ايزيس.
لأنني أفجَع بالصّدى
يعودُ لي مردّداً
دعائيَ الجريح
أحسني توتراً يهفو إلى المسيح.
أخالني شربتُ جرّتي حنان
ينصبّ من عينيهِ في كياني
وأنتشي لأنه افتداني،
وأنتشي
أحسّ في فمي مرارة الدموع.
وظلمةً كثيفةً في ناظري تشيع.
لم يُفدني المسيح
هيهاتِ يستطيع.

يا إخوتي
أنتم رواءُ مُقلتي
صلبتُكمُ
جرحتُكمُ

A Piece of My Innocent Heart

The fingers of regret suffocate me,
uproot me, turn me into a sheet of pain,
because I am innocent
beyond the limits of what my will could bear.
I rise:
I know I crucified my brothers,
my loved ones.
I plead: Odysseus! Odysseus!
You who unearthed our land,
released its chained-up gifts,
be generous. Give me two palms full of your tears.
Wash away my sin.
Lift from my tortured conscience
the pain and burning of my soiling.
Be generous, Odysseus!
Because the echo devastates me,
comes back to me, repeating
my bleeding prayers.
I feel I am agitation—longing for Christ.
I imagine that I drank two draughts of tenderness
poured from his eyes into my soul,
ecstatic that he had sacrificed himself for me.
And then I fold,
taste in my mouth my bitter tears.
Heavy darkness spreads over my eyes.
Christ did not set me free.
I only wished he could.

My brothers:
You quench the thirst of my eyes!
I crucified you.
I mutilated you,

جرحتُ قلبي قبلكم
وحينما تردّ لي ايزيس دَعَواتي لكم
بَسَماتُكم تَهمي على روحي مطر
تَروي بها عُقم الصخر
لعل يوماً تخصَبُ
وعلّ يوماً تهبُّ.

slashed my own heart, then yours.
When Odysseus answers my prayers for you,
your smiles will pour rain on my soul,
quench this parched rock.
Perhaps it will turn green one day.
Perhaps it will flourish again.

I Abandon My Homeland

الرحيل عن الوطن

قرارة موشّح أندلسي

ها قبةٌ خضراءُ
ها قوسُ كبابِ دمشقَ
ساحاتٌ،
ورودٌ من مشاتل سوريَا
لكنّما
اشبيليا، اشبيليا
في قاعةٍ أمويّةِ الأجواءِ
ترفلُ بالحرير
واللحن موجوعٌ أسير
يتسلق العمدان ملهوف الحنين
ويشفّ،
يقطرُ
والهاً
عذباً

حزين.
وعلى العيون
خلف المحاجرِ، في اختلاجاتِ الجفون
الشامُ تولدُ تارةً
الشامُ ثانيةً تموت.
اشبيليا
كتفاكِ عاريتانِ
ما ارتضتا عباءاتٍ يوشّيها القصب،
وسدىً أربتُ وجنتيكِ
بكفِ آتٍ مغترب،
هجرَ الديارَ معلّلًا
أن قد ستولدُ سوريّا
أخرى على إشبيليا
وثنيّةٍ
عيناك قاسيتانِ، ذكرى عن مجامرَ بربريّة.
جئنا لمعبدك الشموخ بحبنا
فعزفتِ عن قُرباننا
صمّاء في وجه المحب، أما تدغدغك الهدّيه؟

Andalusian Song

A green dome,
an arch like the gate of Damascus,
courtyards,
roses from the nurseries of Syria.
But
Seville—Seville is
in a hall with an Umayyad feel,
strolling in silk.
The melody is wounded, hostage,
ascends the columns, yearns impatiently
expands,
drips
enchanted
sweet
sad.
In my head,
behind my eyes, in the trembling of my lashes,
al-Sham is reborn sometimes,
and then she dies again.
Seville,
your shoulders bare,
you refuse to suffer the *abaya*, adorned with threads of gold.
Hopelessly, I stroke your cheeks
with the palm of a returning exile
who abandoned his homeland with the excuse
that a new Syria could be born
in Seville—
pagan
are your cruel eyes, a reminder of the barbaric incense burners.
I came to your proud temple with my love.
You refused my sacrifice,
turned a deaf ear to your lover. Don't my gifts arouse your heart?

يأتيك حامِلُها يُغنّيك الرّجاء
وأنت صامتةً عصيّه؟
ترقصُ الشامُ على قلبي نسيمات خَفايا
- آه ما أحنى -فحتى الميّت تعطيهِ شِغافا.
كلّ مرج عاشقٌ بين يديها
كلّ عينٍ رأت النورَ عليها
مستهامه
وتناغى كل صبٍّ في هواها
أبداً لم تُنكرِ الشامُ فَتاها
لم تقابله بعينٍ حجريّة
تتصبّى الأمسَ جمراً وطقوساً بربريّه.
ويطوفُ ساقينا
كأساً تَلي كأسا
بالوهمِ تُغرينا
وتراوغُ الحِسا
فلعلّنا ننسى
إن كان يُنُسينا
وهمُ ولو حينا.
بردى في العين صبحاً ومساء
يتراءى
كل أحبابي على صفحتِهِ

(ونديمٍ همت في رفقتِهِ
ويُشربِ الراحِ من راحتِهِ)
(كلما استيقظ من غفوتِهِ
جذب الزقَّ اليه واتكا)
فبعيدُ الدار في غربته
إن صحا غنّى وإن غنّى بكى.

The bearer of gifts comes singing, pleading.
Why are you silent, stubborn?
Al-Sham dances in my heart with soft breezes.
How tender she is! Even the dead can feel her affection!
Every meadow is a lover in her hands.
Every eye sees the light in her,
the point of adoration.
Every lover sings her praises,
and al-Sham never rejects her young lover,
never stares at him with stony eyes.
She revives her yesterdays with hot embers and pagan rituals.
Our wine boy goes 'round,
pours cup after cup,
tempts us with illusion,
and deceives our senses
that perhaps we might forget,
if we can be made to forget
with illusions, even if for a time.
The Barada lies in sight morning and evening.
I see all my lovers
on its ripples.
Here with a companion whose company I adore,
and drinking wine from his hand.
Every time he wakes up,
he puts the bottle to his lips, then rests back on his arm.
Far from home in his aloneness,
when he wakes up he sings, and when he sings he cries.

Seville is a city in Spain that flourished during the Arabs' rule of Andalusia, and al-Sham, or the Levant, is the region of greater Syria. The Barada River crosses through Damascus. *'Abaya* here refers to the long dress worn by Arab women.

غجريّة

وحشةُ الليل على العينين تجثُم
ونداءُ الغاب في البُوَيقِ مُبهم.
غجريّة
كعمود النار قدٌ يتلوى
وشفاهُ مُترعاتٌ عنجهيّة.
يا جحيمَ الطبلِ والمزمارِ عُد بي
لعشيّات العصورِ الوثنيّة
عبر عيني غجريّة
رحلتي خلفَ مسافاتٍ قصيّة
خلف ما يرتادُ وهمٌ أو خيال.
غجريّة
قدمٌ تَضربُ صدرَ الأرضِ، تعلو
وتدقُّ الأرض دقًا
زوبعاتٌ من غبار
ودُوار
وعُروقٌ مُجهداتٌ.
تتلظى وَقَدَ نار.
أمطريني
أمطريني
مِن سَديمِ الغيبِ زَخّات سخيّة
ألصقيني بالتراب
أنا مَن خلّف ليلَ المدنيّة
ظامئاً لَم يَسقِني إلا السراب.
حين تكتظّ النوادي بمساخرِ
بدُمى آليةٍ ترقصُ تانجو
يزحفُ الموتُ مع التانجو صَموت
تتلاشى الحيويّة
بخُفوت.
غجريّة
جثثٌ تهوي، تَموت
مثلما ينتفض الطيرُ الذبيح
مثلما تعصفُ بالأوراقِ ريح

A Gypsy

The seduction of night falls heavy on my eyes,
the call of the jungle in my pupil, mysterious.
A gypsy,
like a column of fire, a figure twisting,
lips plump, proud.
Hell of drum and flute! Take me back
to the nights of pagan times
through the eyes of a gypsy.
My journey is beyond far horizons,
beyond the crossings of fiction and imagination.
Gypsy!
Her foot slams the face of earth, rises,
gives the ground a beating.
Sandy storms,
dizziness,
exhausted veins
burning in the heat of fire.
Rain on me!
Rain on me
torrents from your cloud of mystery.
Plant me in the soil.
I who left the city's darkness,
and, thirsty, drank naught but a mirage.
When the clubs crowd with mockery,
with mechanical dolls dancing the tango,
death creeps silently into the tango,
and life disappears
quietly.
Gypsy!
Bodies fall and die,
quiver like slaughtered birds,
like wind shaking leaves

يتهاوون إذا عربدَ جاز.
أيها البوقُ اللعين
أيها الناعق في ليل جموع الميّتين
ليتني أصبحتُ أعمى
وأصمّا
قبل أن أشهد ليل الميتين
غجريّة
هاربٌ يَحملني مدَّ الدروب
قدري الأسودُ مجهولٌ رهيب
وتَناهى بي مطافي
عند عينين هما مقبرتا كلِّ الخوافي.
غجريّة
أنا إن أنحر لعينيكِ ضحيّة
ففؤادي
أمطريني
أمطريني

من سَديم الغيب زخّات سخيّة
أمطريني أنت ما زلت غنيّة
عبقُ الأعشابِ في نهديكِ
والأرض النديّة
لم يُلطِّخ شفتيكِ الطينُ
بنيّاً وأحمر
لم تخونّي منحةَ الشمسِ
فهذا الوجه أسمر
ما كسته حلل الوجه المزوّر.
غجريّة
ما الذي تحمل عينيك من الأسرارِ
ألغاز الحكاية السرمديّة
أنت لا تدرين شيًا
ثورةُ الساقين تدري
عُنفوان النهدِ يدري
وأنا أبحرُ في عينيكِ، أشقى
غير أني لست أدري.

that fall when jazz blasts.
That dreadful trumpet,
hollering through the night into a dead crowd!
Would that I were blind
and deaf
before I witnessed the night of the dead.
Gypsy!
I am running away, carried along by distant roads,
my black faith, unknown, terrifying.
My journey ends
in your eyes, the graveyards of everything mysterious.
Gypsy!
If I make a sacrifice to you,
it will be my heart.
Rain on me!

Rain on me
torrents from your cloud of mystery.
Rain on me! You are still wealthy
with the scent of grass on your breasts,
and the dew drenched earth.
Your lips not soiled with muddy
brown and red.
You have not betrayed the gift of the sun.
This face is tanned,
not made up with the paint of a fake face.
Gypsy!
What secrets do your eyes hold?
The riddles of ancient tales?
But you know nothing.
The riot of your feet knows.
The pride of your breast knows.
I journey through your eyes,
I struggle,
and I know nothing.

عودة إلى الرفاق المتعبين

تسألُ الغابيّةُ السمراءُ عما خلف صمتي
وتعرّيني بنظرة
فأحسُ الحرقة الحَرّى بحلقي
غاصَ نُطقي
أجلد الأحرف موجوعاً أُمزق.
أتحرّق
وأرى عيناً بعينيّ تُحدق
أقبضُ الظلمةَ في كفيّ وأغرق.
غجريّة

يا لهاث الرملِ، يا إنسانيّ الضائعَ
في أصداءِ موالٍ حزين
الحكايات التي ترويّن
في خلجات أعصابي عادت تتململ
عن كليبٍ وجراحاتُ المهلهل
فأعيدي كلَّ ما كان
ولا تَقسي على جسّاس من أجل خيانة
كلنا كان يخون.

آه كلا
لا تقولي!
ليس بي مسُّ جنون
واغفري لي
أترى تغفر ذنباً غجريّة؟

غجريّة
كذبٌ: من قالَ في عينيكِ أسرارُ خفيّة؟
مِثلما تَسعى على الأرضِ الديادين الغبيّة
أنتِ تسعيَن
خواءُ ملءُ عينيكِ بَلاهة
وغباءٌ مطبقٌ يَقعي وسَقمُ وتفاهه
عنفوانُ النهدِ لا يغري

My Return to Tired Comrades

The dark forest girl asks what lies behind my silence,
strips me naked with a glance.
I feel the burning in my throat,
my words fail.
Torn with pain, I churn the alphabet.
Burning,
I see her eye staring at my eye.
I hold her darkness in my palm and drown.
Gypsy!
You are the passion of the sand. The one lost
in the echo of a sad song.
The tales you tell
pulse in my nerves, that quiver again
for Kulaib and the wounds of Muhalhal.
Let us return to all that was
and not be cruel to Jassas for his betrayal.
We all betray someone.

No, no,
don't say
I have no trace of madness
and forgive me.
Can a gypsy forgive my sin?

Gypsy!
Lies: Who said there were secrets hidden in your eyes?
Like the senseless worms crawling along the ground,
you crawl,
empty, eyes full of stupidity,
foolishness, death, and emptiness.
The pride of your breast does not tempt me.
The hunger of your legs does not tempt me.

وجوعُ الساقِ لا يغري
وما في الكهفِ من مكنونٍ سرٌّ
رحلتي كانت ضياعا
فوداعا،
وإذا ما كان أمسي
تافهاً عافته نفسي
وإذا كان مصيري
شاطىءُ الصمتِ الكبيرِ
حيث لا بسمةٌ لا لوعةُ حسره.
يُغرق النسيان ما ضجّ
بنبضِ العرقِ من شكٍ وحَيره
فأنا أطفأت في صدري إلحاحَ السؤال
حين أدركت المآل.

وعَزائي
رفقةٌ لَم يصلبوا جسّاس من أجل خيانة
يسألون الحبَ يعطون محبة
يغفرون
كلنا كان يخون
يا غبيّة
لست إلا غجريّة.

There is no secret hidden in your cave.
My journey was for nothing,
so goodbye.
If yesterday was
worthless, my soul will reject it.
If my destiny is
the great silent shore—
no smile, no torment, no pain.
Forgetting drowns what clamored
in the pulse of my veins with doubt and suspense.
I shut down the nagging question still in my chest
when I realize this is the end.
My solace:
friends who did not crucify Jassas for his betrayal,
they ask for love and they give love—kindness,
they forgive.
We all betray someone.
Stupid girl!
You are nothing but a gypsy.

Jassas was a pre-Islamic poet and warrior who killed his cousin Kulaib, the leader of the tribe, after a call for revenge by Jassas's aunt for the killing of her friend's she-camel. Al-Muhallah is another poet and warrior and Kulaib's brother, who vowed to avenge Kulaib's murder. The incident led to forty years of war among many of the pre-Islamic tribes of Arabia.

المهجورون

يا بريقَ الحبِّ عُد ضَوءَ دُنانا
يا بريقاً هو مِنّا
نحنُ مِنه -تَتَشهّاه رُؤانا.
أنت حيّن انحسرتْ أمواجكَ البيضاءُ
عن شاطيء أحلامِ صِبانا
وتلفَّتنا:
يَبابُ الشطِ والصمتُ مَرير
آه لا رجّةُ مجدافٍ ولا إيماضُ بَسمة،
أه والعصرُ قصير،
نحنُ أدركنا المصير،
فانتحبنا
وتعذّبنا طويلا.
نظراتٍ جَمُدت فوقَ جدار الليلِ
أعصابٌ مُزَيفة
أكبدٌ تُحرقُ في نارِ الحقيقة
نحنُ، نحنُ الأشقياءُ
مرَّ أحبابٌ بنا ألقوا بنظره
وأشاحوا الوجهَ عنا
فدعوناهم بذُعر والتياع.
أبرياءُ نحنُ لكنّا ضحايا الوِّحدةَ
الخُرساءُ والخوفُ المُردّي والضَياع.
يا أحبّانا تعالوا
ليضُمَّ الواحدَ الآخرَ مِنّا
بدِّدوا الوحشة عَنّا.
رُدّت الدعواتُ في أعماقنا السُفلى
وتاهت في مداها
آه ما أقسى صَداها
ونكَصنا نتمنّى
ليتنا عُدنا صغاراً
نَبتني في الشاطىء الرملي بَيت
ليت
لكنّ
ومتى تنفعُ ليت.

The Abandoned

O flash of love! Return light to our world.
O flash of light! You are part of us.
We are part of you. We long for you in our dreams.
You, when your white waves vanished
from the dreams of our youth,
we looked back:
the shores were barren, the silence bitter.
No trembling in the oar, no glow of a smile.
Life is short.
Our destiny caught up with us.
So we wept,
suffered long,
our stares frozen on the wall of night.
Nerves shattered,
our hearts burned with the fire of truth.
We, we the miserable.
Lovers passed by, glanced,
then turned their faces away.
We called out in terror and torment:
We are innocent! The victims of mute
loneliness, of mortal fear, and of emptiness.
Lovers, come!
Let each of us embrace the other
to scatter our loneliness.
This call went out from the depth of our souls
and was lost in the distance.
How cruel the echo sounded.
We came back wishing,
wishing that we might be young again
and build a home at the sandy shore.
We hoped.
      But
             what good is hope?

المستحيل

لا وعمق السرِّ في عَينيكِ ما كان غَراما
وانكفاءاتي ونزفي وأناشيدي اليتامى
لم تَكُن صرخةُ قيسٍ خلفَ ليلى
ففؤادي لم يعد للحُبِّ أهلا،
إنما يَسحَقُ قلبي من قديمٍ، من قديم
سعْيه الدائبُ للوهم وشوقٌ للسَّديم
قبل أن يسمع عن قيسٍ وليلى
كان بعدُ هذا القلبُ طفلا
حينها انسلَّت إليه خلسةً إحدى الليالي
رغبةٌ غامضةٌ ألقتهُ في مَدِّ المُحال
أن يَطول القَمرا
وبكى مذْ شَعَرا
أن سيبقى أبدا في أَسر صدري
بعدها لوَّن بالمأساةِ عُمري.
فإذا هزَّتكِ مني يا صديقه
عبرَ صَمتِ الليل صَرخاتٌ غريقه
فاسمعيها وابك من أجلي ولكن لا تُجيبي
فزهورُ الحب لن تنمو في روحي الجَديب
أنتِ لو جئتِ سينساك فؤادي.

تحت وَقع السَّوط ينشقُّ، يُنادي
يتمنى حُبَّ أُخرى لا تُطال
لن تُخلّيه غوايات المحال
وكفاني أنني سُمِّرتُ-لم أختر-لآلام الصليبِ
فاسمعيني وابكِ من أجلي ولكن لا تُجيبي.

The Impossible

No, I swear by the deep secret in your eyes, it was not love.
My loneliness, my bleeding, my orphan songs
are not the cries of Qais for Layla.
My jaded heart can love no more.
It was crushed long, long ago
by an endless quest for daydreams and longing for stars,
before I ever heard of Qais and Layla.
My heart was still young
when a mysterious desire sneaked into it one night
and cast it into the impossible,
trying to reach the moon.
My heart wept and knew
that it must remain forever in the prison of my chest.
Since then, tragedy stained my life.
If perchance, my friend, you are moved
in the silence of the night by the cries of my drowning,
listen to them, and weep for me. But don't reply.
The flowers of love will not grow in my barren heart.
If you come, my heart will not remember you.

Under cracks of the whip I broke, called out,
begged for the love of one who can't be reached.
I won't be free from the temptations of the impossible.
I was crucified. But I didn't choose the pains of the cross.
Hear me, and weep for me. But don't reply.

Qais and Layla are legendary lovers of Arab folklore. Their love story is frequently
referenced in Sufi traditions, with Qais being *al-majnoun*, the one insanely in love.

My Chaos and Defeat

الفوضى والضياع

رعب

فجّر صخباً
صخباً
صخباً.

حائِر
في زاويةٍ يَقْعي الصمت
الصمت نذيرٌ بالموت
فأَسرع
فأَسرع
أطلق صوت.

شدقاه انفتحا عن هُوّه
بَلعت أجيالاً وعصور
عيناهُ لُهاثٌ مَسعور
وأَدَ الأحلامَ المرجوه
في عينيْ عذراءَ صبيّة
كانت يوماً
وتلاشت ذكرى مطويّة.

صَخَباً
صَخَباً
ألحانُ زنوجٍ ناريّة
قهقهةُ عاهرةٌ الاصداء
مرحى لعجوزٍ شمطاء،
للوحل اللّزج على فمها
لرفاقِ الليلةِ
للبلهاء
ولتُسحق عذراءُ صبيّة.

-كاسٌ أخر
-لحنٌ آخر
-يا ليت الليل بدون نهار.
-نَخبَ الورعين مع الكفار

Terror

Blast! Chaos!
     Chaos.
          Chaos.
Be careful!
In the corner silence spreads,
a warning of death.
Run!
Run!
Make noise!

His mouth opened into a pit,
swallowed generations, centuries,
his eyes rabid, panting,
buried hopeful dreams
in the eyes of a young virgin.
There was one day.
Then it disappeared, a collapsed memory.

Chaos.
Chaos.
Fiery African songs.
Laughter that echoes sin.
Greetings to an old crone,
to the sticky mud on her lips,
to the companions of tonight,
     to these fools.
A time for a young virgin to be crushed.

> *Another cup*
> *Another song*
> *I wish those nights had been without days.*
> *I drank to believers and to infidels.*

-فَرّغ الكأس.

وتَداعت جدرانٌ في الرأس
خَفَت اللحنُ
ومشى في الأرصفة الموتُ.
قَدماه على شفتَي طفلة
تطأَن دعاءً للقُبلة
لم يبلغ أذن مناداه
والآن يمزّقُ نسجَ الصمت
ينشقُّ أمامي شِدقاه
فأضيعُ وما حولي من صوت
لن تُسمع حتى (أَوّاهُ).

I emptied my cups.

Walls in my head crumbled.
The music died.
Death walked the sidewalks,
its boot on the lips of a little girl,
crushing her cry for a kiss
that could not reach the ears of the one she cried for.
Now he rips the fabric of silence,
his mouth wide open before me.
I, and the sound around me, are lost.
You won't hear even my last shriek.

مرثية القافلة الاولى

طلعَ الصباحُ على العيونِ الطيّبة
ومع الظهيره أَطبقت
عشرون ألفاً مطفأة
عشرون ألفَ يدٍ مممددةٍ ولا
دفءَ يوسدُّ امرأة
دع عنكَ قولكَ
في الغَداةِ
النصرُ آتٍ
لا.
الحزنُ ينقضُ نَسجِ قلبي
يمتدّ من قلبي وحتّى
لا نهاية
شَحُبَ الصباحُ
والموتُ لاح
قدراً أخاً
حطَّ الرحال
وتجهّم التاريخُ للشعب الضحوك
ودون جَولة
ذَبَحَ الرجال
أدري بأني لو بكيتُ مصير شعبي
لو أعارتني ثكالى النُوقِ حُنجرة
سدىً
أُزجي لسيناءَ العجوزَ نحيبَ شعبي
لا صدى.
عشرون ألف مقلةٍ
نقرَ العُقابُ
لا تَهذ بالنصر المُلّفَّقِ
إنني أُنبيكَ
خُذ:
النورُ غابَ
والليلُ أطبقَ
فليكن ليلٌ – وكان.

Elegy of the First Caravan

The morning opened on those gentle eyes,
and by noon they were closed.
Twenty thousand lights put out.
Twenty thousand hands outstretched
and no warmth left to put a woman to bed.
Don't say:
Tomorrow
the victory will come!
No.
Sadness shreds the fabric of my heart,
reaches from my heart
to eternity.
The morning bleached white,
death appeared—
a destiny, a brother—
and settled in.
History frowned on a smiling people.
Without a fight,
men were slaughtered.
I know. If I wail for the destiny of my people,
even if the bereaved she-camels lend me their bellowing,
it is useless.
I tenderly send to old Sinai the weeping of my people.
No echo.
Twenty thousand eyeballs
picked out by vultures.
Don't conjure up a false victory.
I am telling you,
believe it:
There was no light there.
The night prevailed.
Let it be night. It is night.

لا

الخيلُ ما صَهَلت على اليرموكِ

لا

والقادسيةُ قصةٌ عجفاءُ

مِن هَذرِ الفرات

فَرَسٌ هُناكَ، وليس غيرَ

تَسيرُ مُطرقةً

تَعثُرُ في العَنان.

فرسُ الهزيمة، ليس غَيره

عشيةَ امتقعَ النهارُ بِذُلَّ شعبي

والليلُ أطبق.

دعْ عنكَ ما يَهذي الجَهول

وما يلفِّقُهُ المُخاتل

الأمرُ في عينيّ ماثل،

الريحُ مثقلةُ هوان

تمضي مع الأبناءِ والأحفاد

تَسري في الزمان

باسمِ الذينَ تَجندلُوا

في أرض سيناء العجوز

زندٌ سيُبرقُ

كفُّ جيلٍ سوف تلتقفُ العَنان

قف

فَرَسُ الهزيمة تَنثني

وحوافرُ الحقدِ الموروِّث

تَنقرُ الامسَ المُبَيّس بالهوان.

سيناءُ

سيناء، يا قلبُ أصمُّ

عليكَ صلى اللهُ ها جسدُ العروبةِ

اسطورةٌ ملأى بتاريخ الجراح

تمدّدت فوق الرمال

إنّا منحناك الهزيمةَ

No.
The horses did not shout victory at Yarmouk.
No.
The story of al-Qadesiyah is a worthless rumor
spread by the chatter of the Euphrates.
One horse left there—nothing else—
wandering with his head down,
tripping on his harness.

The horse of defeat, nothing else.
The evening turned dark with the abasement of my people,
and night prevailed.
Forget the ranting of ignorant men,
forget the lies of demagogues.

It is here in my eyes:
the wind is heavy with shame
blowing over children and grandchildren,
reaching into time.
In the name of those killed
in the land of old Sinai,
one day a wrist will be set aflame,
the hand of a generation will pick up the harness.
Stop!
The horse of defeat bent low,
and the hooves of ancient hatreds
digging up a past hardened by humiliation.
Sinai!
Sinai, you of cold heart!
God prayed over you. The corpse of our Arabism,
a tale, full of a history of wounds,
stretched out over the sand.
We gave you our defeat,

عِزٌّ ما يهبُ الرجال
فليحترق تاريخُ شعبي
إنّا عبرنا الجسرَ
خلفَنا رُكامُ الوردِ والموّال
ذِكرى من نفاياتِ القرون
والطيبونَ المؤمنون
سيناءُ
عَبروا ليغتسلوا بحمّام الدماء.
سيناء يا للموعد الجهريِّ
حيثُ حسابُ شعبيَ الذبحُ
هذي بعدُ أولُ قافلةٍ
فلتَحفظي شرفَ الريادة
في ضمير الرمل سرّا.
حتى إذا شقّت سجوفَ الليل فجرا
تدرينَ أن دماءَنا
زيتٌ يُضيء على منارة
ويقال أنّ هزيمةً
خطَّت إلى الآتي فَخاره
الأمرُ في عينيّ ماثل
وأرى البداية والنهايةَ
لكنَّما
الحزن ينقُضُ نسجَ قلبي
يمتدَ من قلبي وحتى
لا نهاية.

the most precious thing men can give.
Let the history of my people burn.
We crossed the bridge,
left behind a pile of flowers and songs,
memories, the litter of centuries,
and so many kind, righteous ones.
Sinai!
They crossed to bathe in the bloodbath.
Sinai, what a pageant it was,
and the price my people paid was their slaughter.
This, just the first caravan.
So, keep the honor of being the first
a secret in the consciousness of the sand.
One day, when the curtains of night open to dawn,
you will know that our blood
is the oil that lights the minaret.
It will be said that this defeat
mapped for those who came after their pride.
It is here in my eyes,
for I see the beginning and the end.
But . . .
sadness shreds the fabric of my heart,
reaches from my heart
to eternity.

The Battle of Yarmouk (634 AD) marked the fall of the Christian Byzantine Empire to the Muslim Arabs. The Battle of al-Qadesiyah (also 636 AD) resulted in the Islamic conquest of Persia and was key to the conquest of Iraq.

ما لم يُقل عن شهرزاد

شهرزاد
لِمَ أَسْرَتْ بي حَكاياكِ إلى أمسٍ دفين؟
عبرَ سردابٍ مِن الأوهامِ يُفضي لِيقين
إذا بي مثقلٌ أحملُ في جنبيّ سرّا
ليس يُدرى
عن خفيّاتِ لياليكِ الطويلة.
(ألف ليلة
كلَّ ليلة
حلمك الأوحدُ أن تَبقي لِليلة).

قصةٌ تُروى ومذ كنّا صغارا
حَمَلَتنا لأراضي الجنَّ
عبرَ الريحِ والأنواءِ في عرضِ البحار.
وحَببناكِ
حَببناكِ كثيرا
وسهرنا ليلةً في إثر أخرى
لهفةٌ تسألُ عمّا
كان من أمرٍ أخيرا
وعفا من بعد ألفٍ شهريار
ففرحنا.
في بلادي، حيث عيُن الطفلِ والشيخِ سواء
دعوةٌ تحيا على وعدِ انتصار.

شهرزادي
شهرزادي يا صديقه
قيل ما قيل ووحدي
أنتِ أسررتِ إليهِ بالحقيقه
ألفَ ليلة
كُلّ ليلة
حلمكُ الاوحدُ أن تبقي لِلَيلة.
فإذا ما الديك صاح
مُعلناً للكونِ ميلاد صباح

What No One Told Us about Scheherazade

Scheherazade,
why did your tales return me to the forgotten past
through a tunnel of illusions that led to certitude?
They made my heart heavy, loaded down my side with a secret
I couldn't understand
of your long mysterious nights.
For a thousand nights,
            every night
your only hope was to last through the night.

A story told to us since we were young
carried us to the land of genies
through storms and shipwrecks on the sea.
We loved you,
we loved you so,
stayed up, night after night,
eagerly asking:
What happens at the end?
Shahryar pardoned you after a thousand nights.
We were elated!
In my homeland, where the eyes of a child and an old man are the same,
hope feeds on the promise of victory.

My Scheherazade,
my Scheherazade, my friend!
Whatever was said was said.
But you whispered the truth to me:
For a thousand nights,
every night
your only hope was to last through the night.
So when the cock crowed,
announcing to the world the birth of the morning,

نِمتِ والموت سوياً في فراشٍ
ألفَ ليله
غاضَ في عينيكِ إيماضُ التَصبّي
واستوت كلُّ المذاقاتِ
فمرٌّ مثلَ عذبٍ.
بعدها كان وما كان -صباح
أنتِ فيهِ بعض ذكرى عن صبية
أين منها شهرزاد.
شهرزادي
خدعةٌ ضلّلتِ الآذان عُمرا
ورسَت في خاطر التاريخ دهَرا.
أن عفا من بعد الفٍ شهريار
وسنبقى

في بلادي -حيثُ عيُن الطفلِ والشيخِ سواء
دعوةٌ تحيا على وعدِ انتصار
كلما دقَّ على الأفقِ شتاء
نتسلى بحكاياكِ الشجيّه
ونغني لانتصارٍ
لم يكن يوما ولا يرجى انتصار
تحت عيني شهريار

you slept with death in your bed.
For a thousand nights,
the light of youth was extinguished from your eyes,
all flavors became the same flavor,
the bitter like the sweet.
After that, it was morning, but was not.
Only the memories of a young girl,
how different from that was Scheherazade!
My Scheherazade,
this lie deceived the ears for generations,
was fixed in the mind of history for centuries:
Shahryar pardoned Scheherazade after a thousand nights.
So it remains—
in my homeland, where the eyes of a child and an old man are the same,
where hope feeds on the promise of victory.
When winter clouds the horizon,
we entertain ourselves with your passionate tales
and sing about victory—
a victory that never was and never will be,
under the watchful eyes of Shahryar.

Scheherazade, of *The Thousand and One Arabian Nights*, entertained King Shahryar with stories through the nights to avoid being executed at dawn.

Leave Taking

الإستئذان بالرحيل

مرثية الشيخ

1

كان صوتاً شاحباً أعلنَ
أنّ الله أكبر
فحملنا الجسدَ الهشَّ وسِرنا
ثمَّ، فوق الأفق الغربيِّ لاحَ
القرصُ أصفر
سورةُ الاغماءِ شدّت وجههُ العاني
عميقاً
وبدا دغلٌ من الزيتونِ أغبر
فوقفنا
للأصيلِ المُجهد العريانِ ننظُر.

2

إن هذا الهيكل الملآن أصداء
سنيناً ومَرارة
ذا الجبين الناتيء المُشرع للأنواءِ
يُومي بجسارة،
فلنقُل: كان سفينة
مثلتْ أضلاعها للريح في عرض البحار
وتحدّت مُغضب الأمواج والحيتان
عاماً بعد عام،
وتناهت نكهةُ البحرِ وسرُّ البحرِ فيها،
فلنقُل:
داخت أخيراً
وتداعى برجُها الآن
فمالت لتنام.

3

فلنقُل: سيفٌ جليلٌ نائمٌ
قد كان ينهض
ظاميءَ الشفرةِ أبيض
جاب أمداءً

The Old Man's Eulogy

1

A pale voice announced:
Allah-u Akbar! God is Great!
So, we carried the fragile body and walked.
Then, the yellow disc appeared
over the western horizon,
the signs of lifelessness sunk deep
into his tired face,
and he turned as gray as an orchard of dusty olive trees.
So, we stopped,
       stared out at the naked, exhausted dusk.

2

His temple, full of the echoes
of years and bitterness,
a jutting brow displayed in death,
a hint of boldness.
Let us say: He was a ship,
its bow exposed to the wind on the high seas.
It faced the terror of the waves and of the whales
year after year.
It was drenched with the scent of the sea and the secret of the sea.
Let us say:
Finally, it became dazed,
its mast broke.
So, it lay down to sleep.

3

Let us say: The sleeping sword of legends
woke up,
its edge thirsty, gleaming,
traveled long,

وخلّى أثراً
أيّان كان،
وكما يعرف هذا الجمع
لا سيفَ جبان
بَل لقرصانٍ مُغامر
جرّدُوه لتَروا نصلًا مُلوى
ثَلَّمتهُ الحُدثان
أغمِدوه
أنَ يستلقي مُسجّىً في الغِماد،
فى جدار المنزل الأرحب صدراً
علّقوهُ
وليكُن عاليَ النّجاد
حقٌّ بعد اليوم ألّا يُشهرا
أبديّ الصمت يبقى
حاضرا
ليسَ للمسٍّ ولكن
لِيُرى

4

وحَين رنَّ مِعْولٌ
ينهشُ أحشاءَ الصفاه
أصّختُ
مَن يَصرخُ (وافجعتاهُ)
سمعتُ ريحاً
في الذُّرى تولولُ

5

ربما قبلَ عُصور
كان هذا الهيكلُ اليابسُ يوماً
سنديانَة
شمخت تستشرفُ الوديانَ
مدَّت جنباتٍ

and left its traces
          wherever it went.
As this crowd knows,
this was not the sword of a coward,
but of a daring pirate.
Pull it out, you will see its twisting edge
dulled by many battles.
Return it to its sheath,
time for it to lie flat in its sheath.
On the widest wall in the house,
hang it.
          Let it be on full display there.
It has the right never to be drawn again.
It remains in eternal silence,
          present,
not to be touched but
          to be seen.

4
When the shovel shrieked,
splitting the wide, smooth rocks of earth,
my ears opened:
Who is screaming? *O my God!*
I heard the wind
          in the distance howl.

5
Perhaps, centuries ago,
this desolate body was
an oak tree
rising watchful over the valleys
with wide branches.

عشّشت فيها النسور
مِن عَلٍ
فهزّت عَطفَ غُصنٍ مُطمئنّة
ألفُ فأسٍ جرّحتها
قطّعت أوصالَها
سالت نُسوغاً
دون أنّه.
مَدّت القشرة من فوق جراج الكبرياء
عمّرت
لَم تَدرِ كم مرّ على أطرافها صيفٌ
او انقضّ شتاء
هي ذي الآن تَهاوت
بعد ان برّحَها طولُ اعتوار
من شموسٍ وصقيعٍ.
كتلةٌ جرداءُ ملأى
بغضونِ العمرِ
توقيع الزمان
لا تقولوا (لم تكن)
كانت،
وهذا الهيكل اليابسُ
من نَفس الأرومة.
بورك الشيخُ سليلُ السنديان
ذلك الشيخ الذي يغفو
مليئاً بالزمان.

6
يا صديق الرياح
غريبَ المجيءِ
غريب الرواح
مُتعباً بالإباء
ايُ سر سحيق
أنت والكبرياء

The eagles nested there
at the top,
shared the sympathy of a serene branch.
A thousand pecks, wounded it,
cut up its limbs.
Its sap seeped out
        without a whimper.
A crust spread over the wounds of pride,
grew old,
        unaware of how many summers passed over its shadow,
how many winters slipped by.
Here it is now, fallen,
after being afflicted with the years shared
by suns and freezes,
a branch-bare mass full of
the marks of age,
        the signatures of time.
Don't say: *It was not.*
It was,
and this shriveled body
is from the same essence.
God bless the old man, the son of oak.
That old man that fell asleep,
full of time.

6

O friend of the wind!
Stranger when you come,
stranger when you leave,
decked with dignity,
what a deep mystery
you and your pride are.

آن أن ترحلا
فالمسا ينتظر
والشجر
مدَّ أيديه عاشقاً
سائلًا
أن تعود
لنسوغِ الجدود.

It is time for you to leave.
The evening is waiting.
The trees
extend their hands in longing,
      asking that
           you return
                 to the pride of our ancestors.

بلا عنوان (1)

1

حقله النائم في صمت الظهيره
سادرٌ عن ذكره
ترقُص الاشواكُ والأرياح فيِه
والجنادبُ
لا تُبالي أنّ ظلَّ الشيخِ غائبُ.
مُلكهُ عاد سبيّه
هِي ذي الصيفيةُ الأولى عليه
ما تبقَّى منها إلا
نقلةٌ في خاطري
جدُّ خفيّة

2

لست أرثِيه وإنّي
خاطري مُرُّ
ويَعصاه الكلام
إنّما
أعرفهُ حقاً كريحِ الفجرِ يَقِظه.
وأرى
الآن الختاما
أطبق الجفنَ ونام
أسِفا
وا أسفاهُ
الفتى الطائشُ قلبي
باتَ يشتاق السلام.

Without a Title (1)

1

His field sleeps through the silence of noonday
dazed, not remembering him.
The thorns and the wind dance therein,
and the grasshoppers
care less that the shadow of the old man is absent.
What he owned turned barren.
The first summer since he's gone passes,
nothing left of it except
a turn within my mind,
      very subtle.

2

I'm not eulogizing him.
My memories are bitter,
      refuse to speak,
      but
      I knew him well, alert, like the morning wind.
Now, I see
      the end.
He closed his eyelids and went to sleep.
Sorry
      How sorry I am
that my foolish heart
started yearning for peace.

أحزان صحراوية (3)

كنتُ قد ألمحت من قبل
مراراً
أن هذا الحزن -حين انسلَّ
محمولًا على ريح الصحارى
قد تناهى
لحنايانا العميقة
حالُنا -حيَّن ألفناهُ – أسارى.
وقديماً
خلتُ ذاكَ القادمَ السرِّي شيخاً
مثل جدّي
وجديراً بالولاء
ولكم حاذرتُ أن أوذي سلامه
وأرى اليومَ بأني
عبرَ تاريخٍ من الهمسِ المحاذر
غاضَ منيِّ الصوتُ إلا
رجفةُ الريح المسافر.
أنني قد أقفز الآن على جُنحِ التفاته
فأرى الطوفانَ
يجتاح الجزيرة
أنني أركض -ألغي الربعَ الخالي
عسيراً، وتُهامه
(فرحةُ الماء بصدري
غسلت منه القَتامة).
ثم أعدو. يحسُر الماء -وأنمو
أخضرَ العود مع الغابات
في عيدِ النّماء
إنني الثلجُ
وأسّاقطُ أبيضَ
وأمتدُّ بعيداً
إنني سرُّ الشتاء
وربيعاً أصبحُ العاشقَ
والطفلَ الذي يلعبُ

Desert Sorrows (3)

I have hinted before
many times
that this sadness—set loose
and carried on the desert wind—
reached
      our inner core
and we became its prisoners when we grew accustomed to it.
In the past,
I imagined a mysterious visitor, an old man,
like my grandfather,
worthy of my loyalty.
How careful I was not to disturb his peace.
I see today that I,
through a life of careful whisper,
lost my voice except for
the trembling of the blowing wind.
I turn my head, and I can fly. With a glance,
I see the flood
sweeping all of Arabia.
I run—wash away the Empty Quarter
and Assir and Tuhama.
The joy of the water fills my chest
      washes away its gloom.
Then I run—the water recedes—and I grow
green limbs like the forest
at the festival of renewal.
I am the snow
falling, white,
stretching far.
I am the secret of winter.
In spring, I become the lover,
and the child at play,

والشيخَ وفي جيبي جريدة.
غيرَ أني بالتفاتة
عائداً من رحلةِ الوهمِ السعيدة
أَلمحُ الشيخَ المُعنّى في إهابي
(دونما حتى جريدة)
لستُ طوفاناً
ولم يخضرّ عودي
لم أكن ثلجاً
ولم أمتدّ في الأمداءِ
شيخاً يُكثرُ القولَ
يُسلّي النفسَ عن هذا وذاك
بحكاياتٍ
قديماتٍ
بذكرى
وقعُها في النفس أَسيانُ
كريحٍ عبرَ صحرا.

and the old man with a newspaper in my pocket.
But with another turn:
I return from the happy journey of illusion,
find the old man in agony filling my footsteps
(without even a newspaper).
I am not a flood
      and my limbs did not green.
I have never been snow
      and did not spread over the distances.
I am an old man who talks too much,
entertains himself with this and that,
with fairy tales—
    old,
        with a memory,

its effect on the soul sadness,
like the wind across the desert.

The Empty Quarter, a vast barren desert in the Arabian Peninsula.
Assir and Tuhama are regions of the Arabian Peninsula.

بلا عنوان (2)

أنا يا صديقي
أسير-مع الوهم أدري
أُيِّمُ نحو تخوم النهاية
نبياً غريب الملامح أمضي
إلى غير غاية.
سأسقطُ، لا بدّ، يملأُ جوفي الظلام
نبياً، قتيلاً وما فاهَ بعدُ بأَيه
وأنتَ صديقي،
وأعلم، لكن قد اختلفت بي طريقي
عُذَيرُك، بعدُ
إذا ما التقينا بذات منام
تُفيق الغداةَ وتنسى
لكم أنت تنسى
عليك السلام.

Without a Title (2)

My friend, I
walk in a dream, aware
wander toward the edge of death.
A strange prophet I am, who left
with no destination in mind.
I will fall. Darkness will no doubt fill my soul,
a dead prophet, who has yet to reveal a verse.
You are my friend,
I know, but my path has changed.
I ask your forgiveness, just in case
we ever meet in a dream.
But you will rise the next day and forget.
How often you forget!
Peace Be Upon You.   • 131

This poem was written in 1973 and was found on Tayseer al-Sboul after his suicide.

الشواطئ الأخيرة

ولعينيك اللَّحونُ المتعبة
منهما جمعتُ معناي وفي
تيههما كان ضياعي.
لَستُ أشكو فلقد شارفتُ شطآن السآمه
بَرَدَت لهفةُ شوقي والتياعي
مَاتت الأضواءُ في عينيَّ
لا وَمضَ شُعاعٍ
لا غوىً أخضرَ
لا لونَ سوى بعضَ قتامة
تتلاشى وأنا أعبرُ أيامي لشطآن السآمه.
ولعينيكِ اللَّحونُ المُتعبة
ولعينيكِ ثُمَالات عَطائِي
سَادرٌ في حُلم عينيك بقائي
وإذا ذلَّلتا يوماً إبائِي

فَعَزائِي
أن في عينيكِ أمطاراً وألوانَ شتاء
وأنا قلبيَ يَباب
وأنا والشمسُ تُلغيني
فأغدو كالسراب
أتفيّا بين عينيكِ
وأشتاق الضَّباب
ويؤدّي اللحنُ في عَظمي:
(هنا يحلو الزَّوال
ألقٌ أبيضُ صافٍ لا يُطال
يحضُنُ الأسودَ
والأسودُ في الأعماق أرخى ثِقلَه غير مُبَال
وبعيداً تَرتَمي الضوضاءُ
في كهفٍ من العالم لا تُعنى به عيناكِ
لا أُعنى به .. جدُّ بعيد).
نظرةٌ في أفق عينيكِ وتنهدُ الحدود
بارتخاءه،
عندما يسبُلُ جفناك وتمتصُ أهداب الشرود

The Final Shore

To your eyes, I sing my tired songs,
from them I gather meaning,
and in their depths I am lost.
No complaint, I reach the shore of boredom,
cool my longing and my pain—
no light in my dead eyes,
no sparks in my gaze,
no green temptation,
no color. But some of the gloom
vanishes when I cross from my days to the shore of boredom.
For your eyes are my tired songs,
to your eyes I give my drunken offering.
I am lost. In the dreams of your eyes, I find me.
If my pride is abased one day,
my solace is this:
In your eyes are rain and colors of winter.
My heart is barren.
The sun erases me,
turns me into a mirage.
I find shade in your eyes
and long for the fog.
The song in my bones sings:
Here death is joy:
A pure, white glimmer that can't be touched
embraces the black.
Blackness at the bottom relaxed, indifferent.
The clamor continues far away,
in a world your eyes don't see or care about,
that I don't care about—so far away.
One look at the horizon of your eyes, boundaries collapse,
your eyes half closed.
Your eyelids shut, resting those wild lashes.

ينثني المدّ بصدري
وفيافٍ تفتحُ الأبعادَ
تُقصيها. وتُقصي مِن جديد
وانتباهَه،
يومضُ البرقُ
يضجُّ الموجُ
يرتجُّ الوجودْ
مرفأً عينيك أنسَى الموحشَ التائَه
يوماً تعبه
لهما منه عُصاراتِ اللحونِ المُتعبة.
طالما غنّى لعينيكِ
ولم يزعم عطاء
وهو يدري أنه من

فيض عينيكِ قد امتاحَ الغناء
موهَن الساعد يمضي
عبرَ بحرٍ من سخاء
سامحيه
واغفري إنَّ عذاب الحرفِ
يُلقي في الشرايين العياء.
واذكري أن اللحون المتعبة
آخر القطف قُبيل الانتهاء.
أوشكَ الملاحُ أن يُلقى لشطآن السآمة
أي شيطانَ.
هنا العمر لا شيء
سوى صمتِ انتظار
وبلا ماضٍ ولا مستقبلٍ
محض انتظار
كلُّ حبٍ
كلُّ ذكرى
ترتمي حتى القرار
وهدوءٌ في القرار
يعبرُ الملاحُ مخذولًا لشطآن السآمه

My chest folds.
Deserts open to the horizon
stretch far, then stretch far again.
She looks up!
Lightning flashes,
waves rise high,
the world trembles.
The shore of your eyes will make one lost and lonely forget
his tiredness.
To them is the essence of his tired songs offered up.
He often sings to your eyes,
never claims your favor,
realizes that from the flow
of your eyes, he scoops his songs.

With tired arms, he moves
into a sea of generosity.
Excuse him, and forgive
the torment of the letters
grinding in his tired veins.
Remember, his tired songs are
the last harvest before the end.
The mariner is almost cast on the shore of boredom,
any shore.
There, life is nothing
but silent waiting,
no past, no future,
mere waiting.
Each love,
each memory,
falls to the bottom,
to serenity at the bottom.
The disappointed mariner crosses over to the shore of boredom.

فدعي يا أنتِ، يا أنتِ الملامة
لستُ أبكي لعذابِ الصلبِ: مرحى لصليبي،
أنا أبكي محنةَ الوحشةِ في صدرِ الغريبِ
حينما لحتِ مع الجلادِ
تُلغيني إذن عيناكِ؟
أغدو كالسراب؟
في ضمير الكونِ شلَّ البوحُ وانهدَّ نشيج
سُدّتِ الدرب فلا حلم دخولٍ أو خروج
آه، آه الجدبُ يقتاتُ المروج.
ورمى الملّاحُ لليمِّ شراعه
كانت الخيبةُ ترتادُ جبينه
ونأى.
رحلةً نحو ضفافٍ دونَ حبٍ أو ضغينة
وبلا ماضٍ ولا مستقبلٍ: محض انتظار
لا تلومي
لا تلومي
أغلقتُ كل دروبي
فلتكن درب الفرار.

136 •

Stop! Stop your blaming!
I don't fear the agony of crucifixion: I welcome my cross.
I weep for the pain and loneliness in the heart of the stranger.
When you appeared with the assassin,
did your eyes erase me?
Did I turn into a mirage?
In the mind of the universe, frozen confessions, sad and silent wailing.
The road is closed, no hope of going in or out.
Look! Barrenness consumes the fields.
The mariner throws his sails into the sea.
Disappointment lingers on his forehead,
and he leaves.
A trip to shores without love, without hate,
no past, no future, only waiting.   • 137
Don't blame me.
Don't blame me.
I closed off all other paths.
Let this be my path of escape.

الرحلة

هو لايذكر شيئاً عن عذاباتِ الليالي الماضيةْ
تّمت الرحلةُ
والوعد على القمةِ
والقمةُ لاحت دانية.
لحظةٌ
طَرفَةُ عين
هي ذي القمة تبدو
ويَرى
لم يكن ثمةَ شيءٌ ليراهُ
لم يكن ثمة شيءٌ ليمسَّه
فإذا القمةُ جداً خاوية
لم يعد يحتاجُ إنساناً
ولا شيئاً
ولا يحتاج جِسمَّه.
واحداً يَمثُلُ، لا يدري إذا كان وحيداً
واحداً يسمعُ لغْط الريح
والصحراءُ في عينيهِ تمتدُّ – وتمتدّ بعيدا
ضجراً كان، وما كان تعيساً أو سعيدا.
أو لعلَ الأمرَ لم يحدث
لعلَ الرحلةَ المومأ إليها لم تكن
والمسألةُ
حلمٌ مرّ طويلًا وثقيلًا وبليدا
كان في القمةِ والقمة جداً باردة،
وإذا ما ارتجّت أوصالُه قد يتذكر
خبراً عن رحلةٍ هابطةٍ
أو صاعده.

The Journey

He remembered nothing of the pain of past nights.
His journey came to an end.
The promise was on the summit,
and the summit loomed near.
A moment,
the twitch of an eye,
and there the summit appears.
He sees
there is nothing there to see.
There is nothing there to touch.
The summit is just empty.
He no longer needs people.
He needs nothing.
He does not need his senses.
One appears. He doesn't know if he is alone.
One listens to the chatter of wind,
and the desert in his eyes stretches—stretches far.
Bored he is, not sad or happy.
Or, perhaps this never happened.
Perhaps the journey never happened,
and it was all
a dream that passed—long, heavy, and dreary.
He is at the summit, and the summit is very cold.
When his limbs shiver, he might remember
what happened on the way down,
or on the way up.